D & S
VOL. 43

ALL NEW EDITION

F-4C, F-4D & RF-4C PHANTOM II

in detail & scale

Bert Kinzey

Airlife Publishing Ltd.

England

 Published by Kalmbach Publishing Company, 21027 Crossroads Circle, P. O. Box 1612, Waukesha, Wisconsin 53187.

CONTRIBUTORS AND SOURCES:

Mick Roth	Don Spering/AIR
Wayne Wachsmuth	Flightleader
Jim Rotramel	McDonnell Douglas
Mike Ashmore	National Archives
George Cockle	Robins AFB Museum of Aviation
Bill Paul	U. S. Air Force Museum
Jim Galloway	U. S. Air Force

Detail & Scale and the author express special appreciation to BG James F. Brown, USAF, former commander of the 117th Tactical Reconnaissance Wing, for his help and cooperation during the preparation of this book.

A special thanks is also extended to Mr. Bob Williams at the McDonnell Douglas Photo Lab for his assistance

Most photographs in this publication are credited to their contributors. Photographs with no credit indicated were taken by the author.

FIRST PRINTING

Published in United States by
Kalmbach Publishing Co.
21027 Crossroads Circle
P.O. Box 1612
Waukesha, Wisconsin, 53187

Library of Congress Cataloging-in-Publication Data

Kinzey, Bert.
F-4C, F-4D & RF-4C Phantom II : in detail & scale /
Bert Kinzey. -- All new ed.
p. cm. -- (D & S ; vol. 43)
"A Detail & Scale aviation publication."
Includes bibliographical references.
ISBN 0-89024-204-6
1. Phantom (Fighter planes) I. Title. II. Title:
F-4C, F-4D and RF-4C Phantom II.
UG1242.F5K52623 1994
623.7'464--dc20 94-5175

Published in Great Britain
by Airlife Publishing Ltd.
7 St. John's Hill, Shrewsbury, SY1 1JE

British Library Cataloging in Publication Data

Kinzey, Bert
F-4C, F-4D & RF-4C Phantoms
in Detail and Scale
1. Phantom II (Fighter Plane)
I. Title.
623.74'64 UG1242.F5
ISBN 0-84310-640-2

Front cover: Among the last F-4Ds in service was 66-7765, which was assigned to the 906th TFG at Wright Patterson Air Force Base. It is shown here in the two tone gray paint scheme with special markings to help celebrate the Phantom's thirtieth birthday. The aircraft originally had markings on the nose for the London, Ontario, International Air Show, but these were later changed to the Dayton Air and Trade Show. However, all of the other thirtieth anniversary markings remained the same. Earlier, when it was painted in the European 1 camouflage scheme, the 906th TFG gave the author a ride in this aircraft. It was during that flight that the rear cover photograph and other photos for <u>Colors & Markings of the F-4D Phantom II</u> were taken.

Rear cover: Details and colors in the front cockpit of an RF-4C are shown in this photograph that was taken shortly after the aircraft returned from Operation Desert Storm.

INTRODUCTION

One of the Air Force's early test and evaluation Phantoms is shown loaded with M117, 750-pound bombs. Note that the multiple ejector racks on the outboard wing pylons are angled slightly to the outside in order to provide maximum clearance between the bombs and the landing gear. This is not due to the angle of the cameral lens, but was standard practice when carrying MERs on the outboard pylons. This mounting angle for the outboard MERs can also be seen in several other photographs in this publication. *(National Archives)*

In 1978, the Detail & Scale Series was started with the idea of producing an ongoing series of aviation monographs that would be unlike any published before. The focus of this new series would be the many physical details of the aircraft such as cockpit interiors, radars and avionics equipment, weapon systems, engines, landing gear, and other features. It was anticipated that serious scale modelers would make up a large segment of the readers, therefore the Detail & Scale Series also featured a modeler's section in the back of each book. This section provided accurate reviews of the model kits that were available on the aircraft that the book covered, and it also listed after-market decals that could be purchased.

After six small books in this format were released, the new series of publications became so successful that Detail & Scale joined forces with Aero Publishers in 1981 to expand the series. At that time the size of each book was increased to seventy-two pages, and the basic format was formalized. Volume 1 in this new format was on the F-4C, F-4D, and RF-4C Phantoms, and several printings sold out before the color separations were lost. This loss meant that the book could no longer be reprinted, so it went out of print in 1985. Since then, Detail & Scale has received numerous requests to do new color separations and to reissue the book.

Much has changed since that first volume on the F-4C, F-4D, and RF-4C was published. Both the F-4C and F-4D have been retired from Air Force service, and as this is written, the few remaining RF-4Cs are flying their last missions with the Air National Guard. RF-4Cs participated in Operations Desert Shield and Desert Storm and provided valuable information on Iraqi installations, troop move-

ments, and battle damage assessment. After more than a quarter-of-a-century of service, the RF-4Cs are now being retired without any new dedicated tactical reconnaissance aircraft to replace them.

There have also been many changes with respect to building scale models of these three variants of the Phantom. Many new kits have been released since our first volume was published. Most of the older kits that were reviewed in the original book are today best left to the collectors, because much better models are now available.

Considering the numerous changes that have been made regarding both the actual aircraft and the scale models, it seemed more appropriate to do a new volume on the F-4C, F-4D, and RF-4C rather than to do a revised edition of the original book, and this is what we have done. The 1/72nd scale, five-view drawings, which were drawn specifically for Volume 1, were excellent, and we have used them again in this publication with one update that pertains to the AN/ALR-69(V)-2 RHAW modification on the F-4D's radome fairing. Otherwise, this is a completely new publication to include photo selection, captions, text, and kit reviews.

The majority of the modeler's section is used to review the new kits that have been released since 1981. Some of the better older models are also included with detailed commentary, but those that are now considered to be collectors' items are only covered with brief reviews.

With new photography, informative captions, and a concise text, this publication will be of interest not only to readers who missed Volume 1, but it will also be valuable to those who have that book in their reference files.

HISTORICAL SUMMARY

Air Force involvement with the Phantom began when it "borrowed" two F-4Bs from the U. S. Navy for testing. Originally designated F-110A by the Air Force, the Phantom proved to be superior to the F-105 Thunderchief as a fighter-bomber and a better air superiority fighter than the F-106 Delta Dart. (National Archives)

In July 1946, an FH-1 Phantom made aviation history aboard the USS FRANKLIN D. ROOSEVELT, CVB-42, when it became the first jet fighter ever to take off from an aircraft carrier. This original Phantom was a twin-engine, straight wing design built by the McDonnell Aircraft Corporation of St. Louis, Missouri. Although McDonnell had primarily been a sub-contractor during World War II, the development of the FH-1 Phantom allowed the fledgling company to get in on the ground floor when it came to designing and producing carrier-based jet fighters. But this may not have been much cause for celebration in the late 1940s, because the future of carrier aviation did not look very promising at that time.

As the U. S. Navy entered the 1950s, there were two major factors that threatened the future of aircraft carriers. One of these was the emphasis on nuclear armament. Military planning during the early days of the Cold War focused on the capability to deliver nuclear weapons against enemy targets and to defend North America from similar weapons delivered by any adversary. For quite some time, it did not appear that aircraft carriers would be able to perform either of these tasks. However, as the development of nuclear weapons progressed, new types were produced that were small and light enough to be employed by fighter and attack aircraft. Soon, aircraft as small as the Douglas A4D Skyhawk could deliver nuclear weapons from the decks of aircraft carriers. While this contribution to the nation's nuclear delivery capability was far less than that of the Strategic Air Command, it was still important. At that time the first inter-continental ballistic missiles were still under development, and there were no submarines with nuclear tipped missiles lurking beneath the oceans. Deploying nuclear weapons aboard carriers therefore helped to disperse the weapons, and it gave the Soviets something else to think about, thus increasing the credibility of deterrence. While this helped to justify the strategic value of aircraft carriers, the Korean War dramatically illustrated that the role carriers could play in conventional warfare was also still very important.

With the need for aircraft carriers re-established in both nuclear and conventional warfare, the other threat to their future still remained. This was the problem of adapting jet aircraft for carrier use. Catapults were mandatory for launching jets, and stronger arresting gear had to be designed. Space aboard carriers had to be made for jet fuel as well as gasoline for aircraft with piston engines. But the even greater challenge was to design jet aircraft that could operate from ships and still offer acceptable performance figures. Most important was the necessity to have the aircraft fly slow enough to land safely aboard a ship.

McDonnell Aircraft Corporation improved upon the FH-1 Phantom with the F2H Banshee. The Banshee also had two engines and a straight wing, but it had better performance than the Phantom. It served alongside the F9F Panther aboard Navy carriers during the Korean War albeit in far fewer numbers than its Grumman contemporary. Neither of these Navy jet fighters was equal to the Air Force's swept-wing F-86 Sabre, which was the premier fighter of that time. More importantly, the Panther and the Banshee were no match for the Soviet MiG-15. Even after the war ended in 1953, it appeared that design considerations for carrier-based fighters would cause them to remain far less capable than their land-based counterparts.

Along with advancements and refinements in aircraft design, it was the development of the FORRESTAL class of super carriers that finally permitted considerable advances in carrier-based jet fighter development. Among the important design features of the super carrier were the steam catapult and the angled landing area. Both of these features were also added to older carriers of the ESSEX and MIDWAY classes, allowing them to effectively operate new jet aircraft as well.

At the same time the Navy was planning improvements to its carriers, a number of aircraft manufacturers were developing the first generation of swept-wing jet fighters that could operate aboard ships. Grumman's first answer was simply to replace the Panther's straight wing with a swept one, and this resulted in the F9F Cougar. Later, Grumman would produce the F11F Tiger as well. Douglas Aircraft Corporation used a modified delta wing on its F4D Skyray, and North American drew on its experience with the F-86 to produce a "navalized" version of

Wearing a large Tactical Air Command insignia and lightning bolt on its tail, 149405 was one of the original two Navy F-4Bs loaned to the Air Force for test and evaluation. These aircraft, along with twenty-seven additional F-4Bs and the first production F-4Cs, were painted in the Navy's standard light gull gray over white paint scheme. The aircraft is shown here "armed" for the air superiority mission with dummy Sidewinder and Sparrow missiles. (National Archives)

the Sabre. Chance Vought's first swept wing fighter was the F7U Cutlass, and at McDonnell the F3H Demon replaced the Banshee on the production line. While all of these aircraft offered increased performance over the Panther and the Banshee, none was entirely successful, and they all fell short of the capabilities offered by the new line of "Century Series" fighters being developed by the Air Force.

While the F7U Cutlass was arguably the least successful of the first generation of swept-wing fighters developed for the Navy, Chance Vought followed it with the F8U Crusader, and for the first time the Navy had a carrier-based fighter that was equal to the land-based aircraft then in operation with the Air Force. Parity in jet fighter design had finally been reached.

At McDonnell, it was obvious that the Crusader offered a substantial increase in performance over the underpowered F3H Demon, so engineers began work on a new design. Originally intended to be an attack aircraft, the single-seat, twin-engine design included provisions for four internal 20mm cannon and external hardpoints for a variety of weapons.

After receiving a formal development proposal from McDonnell in August 1954, the Navy gave the go-ahead for the production of a mock-up and two prototype aircraft. The designation AH-1 was selected to reflect the design's intended ground attack mission. However, before the prototypes were ever built, the Navy and McDonnell agreed to several changes, including a two-place cockpit with the seats arranged in tandem. The addition of the radar-guided Sparrow III air-to-air missile justified the change in designation to F4H-1.

Many additional modifications to the design were incorporated before the first prototype finally took to the air on 27 May 1958. After some problems were worked

out, the Navy conducted a fly-off between the F4H-1 and the F8U-3 Crusader at Edwards Air Force Base. Both aircraft proved to be outstanding, but budget constraints meant that only one could be put into production. The F4H-1 was chosen, and the F8U-3 became known as the best aircraft design ever cancelled. Impressed with the F4H-1, which had by now been named the Phantom II, the Navy and McDonnell set up a series of demonstrations to publicize the aircraft's amazing capabilities. To the astonishment of the aviation world, altitude, speed, and time-to-climb records were shattered by an aircraft that was designed to operate from the decks of aircraft carriers.

Shortly after the Phantom began to enter service with the Navy, John F. Kennedy became President of the United States after winning a narrow victory over Richard Nixon. President Kennedy appointed Robert McNamara as his Secretary of Defense, and McNamara set out to realign and redefine the U. S. Department of Defense. While standing on the superstructure of one of the new super carriers to observe a fly-by of the various aircraft in the ship's air wing, McNamara asked, "Why do we need all of those different types of planes?" Under the concept of commonality, McNamara wanted to develop one plane that would perform a wide variety of missions for both the Air Force and the Navy. While this would later result in the F-111 program, McNamara realized that the F4H was clearly the best fighter in the U. S. inventory, and directed that the Air Force evaluate the Phantom for its own use.

At that time, the F-105 Thunderchief was the best fighter-bomber operational with the U. S. Air Force. The "Thud" was a fine aircraft, but its design was more oriented to the "bomber" side of the spectrum. It could deliver nuclear weapons from an internal bomb bay while traveling at supersonic speeds right down on the deck. It

F-4B, 149406, was the second of the original two Navy Phantoms evaluated by the Air Force. In contrast to 149405 shown above, this aircraft is loaded with M117, 750-pound bombs. This is the same F-4B that is illustrated on the previous page with the F-110 designation on the nose. However, this designation was short lived and was soon removed from the aircraft as seen here. (National Archives)

The Air Force subsequently received twenty-seven more F-4Bs from the Navy. Several of these aircraft can be seen in this photograph. Like the original two F-4Bs, these Phantoms were also painted in the light gull gray over white scheme. **(National Archives)**

also could carry an impressive amount of conventional air-to-ground ordnance, but its abilities in aerial combat were limited by its poor maneuverability and lack of sophisticated air-to-air weapons. The Phantom could not only carry an equal or greater weapons load to attack ground targets, it also possessed an excellent ability to engage enemy aircraft with its Sparrow missiles. This multi-mission capability was exactly what McNamara and the Air Force wanted.

Operation Highspeed, which was conducted in 1961, evaluated the Phantom against the new F-106 Delta Dart in the air-to-air role. In a few respects, the "Six" was better than the Phantom, but the overall superiority of the Phantom was clearly established. It was also simpler to maintain, and its weapons were more reliable.

In January 1962, the Air Force "borrowed" two Phantoms from the Navy for 120 days of intensive testing and evaluation. Still painted in the Navy's gray over white scheme, each aircraft had TAC insignia and lightning bolts emblazoned on its vertical tail. The original Air Force designation, F-110A, was lettered boldly on each side of the nose. Before the evaluation was finished, commonality had even reached the system for designating military aircraft. The existing Navy and Marine Phantoms became F-4As and F-4Bs, while the designation F-110 was changed to F-4C.

With the evaluation complete, the Air Force issued Specific Operation Requirement 200 including the changes that it wanted incorporated into its first production version of the Phantom. Most important among these was the capability to deliver a wide variety of air-to-ground ordnance ranging from napalm to nuclear weapons. The ability to employ the Navy's Bullpup air-to-ground missile was likewise included, and the infrared guided AIM-4D Falcon air-to-air missile was to supplement the radar guided Sparrows. The Air Force added flight controls and side consoles to the rear cockpit, and assigned a rated pilot to the Phantom's rear seat. Larger tires were specified for the main landing gear, and stronger brakes were incorporated in the wheels. This change necessitated the addition of bulges in the upper and lower wing panels and in the main landing gear doors so that the wells would be deep enough to accommodate the wider wheels and tires when the gear was retracted. This change also appeared on later Navy variants of the Phantom as well.

General Electric J79-GE-15 engines replaced the -8 versions used in Navy Phantoms, this change being dictated by the Air Force's desire to have an engine with a self-starting capability. To make the aircraft more compatible with Air Force tankers, the Navy style refueling probe was removed from the forward right side of the fuselage and was replaced with a receptacle for the high-speed boom system in the spine of the aircraft. The AN/APQ-100 radar replaced the AN/APQ-72 used in the F-4B.

While the Air Force waited for delivery of its first F-4Cs, twenty-seven more F-4Bs were obtained from the Navy. Most of these aircraft were assigned to the 4453rd Combat Crew Training Wing at MacDill AFB, Florida, where the Air Force began to form the cadre of personnel that would train its first Phantom pilots, weapon systems officers, and maintenance personnel.

Five years to the day after the first Phantom made its initial flight, the first F-4C took off from Lambert Field on 27 May, 1963. It exceeded Mach 2 on its maiden flight, and was immediately accepted by the Air Force. As more F-4Cs came off the production line, most were assigned to the 4453rd CCTW to replace the F-4Bs. Others were used for continued testing and evaluations as well as for weapons certification. Beginning in January 1964, the F-4Cs were assigned to the 12th TFW at MacDill AFB, and this unit became combat ready with the Phantom the following October. Early the next year, F-4Cs were flying combat missions in Southeast Asia. More information about the F-4C can be found beginning on page 9.

Realizing that the Phantom's large airframe and powerful engines offered a far greater capability than the F-4C delivered, the Air Force studied a wide range of proposals that contained possible improvements to the aircraft. Some optimized the air-to-air capabilities, while others concentrated on upgrading air-to-ground performance. But the Air Force selected a proposal that promised improvements in both areas, and the resulting F-4D was ordered by a letter contract in March 1964.

The first flight of an F-4D took place on 8 December, 1965, and the first sixteen aircraft were assigned to the Fighter Weapons School at Nellis, AFB, Nevada. Shortly thereafter, the 33rd TFW at Eglin AFB, Florida, became the first combat unit to receive the new Phantom variant. By the middle of 1967, the Air Force was replacing F-4Cs with F-4Ds in the squadrons that were flying combat missions in Southeast Asia. The rapid deployment of the new F-4Ds to a combat environment precluded extensive testing, and as a result there were some early operational problems with the aircraft and its systems. Most of these were solved as time went on, and lessons learned in combat resulted in numerous improvements and modifi-

In Vietnam, Phantoms were tasked with keeping the skies clear of enemy aircraft. Loaded with AIM-9 Sidewinder and AIM-7 Sparrow air-to-air missiles, this F-4D is about ready to taxi out to the runway for a mission over North Vietnam. The star on its intake ramp symbolizes an earlier victory over a communist MiG. (National Archives)

cations. Significant among these was the F-4D being used as the first aircraft to employ laser and electro-optically guided "smart" bombs.

But Vietnam was not the only place in the world where the Air Force had commitments. F-4Ds were also assigned to units in Europe. USAFE Phantoms stood alert with nuclear weapons to deter the Soviet Union and Warsaw Pact nations from invading Europe. Others were ready to repel any attack from the air or on the ground with conventional weapons. With the Phantom, the Air Force truly had a multi-mission aircraft that was ready to respond to any threat in the European Theater of Operations (ETO) or elsewhere in the world. More information on the F-4D can be found beginning on page 14.

In addition to its air-to-air and conventional ground attack missions, the Phantom was also used by the Air Force to stand nuclear alert with tactical nuclear weapons. Here an F-4D is shown in a shelter in Europe with a nuclear weapon attached to its centerline station. An ECM pod is on the right inboard pylon. (National Archives)

The Air Force also realized the Phantom's potential as a tactical reconnaissance aircraft and developed the RF-4C variant. The fourth RF-4C is shown here, and it is fitted with an instrumentation probe for testing. The Navy also ordered the RF-4B version for use with the Marine Corps. *(National Archives)*

Early in its evaluation of the Phantom, the Air Force realized that the F-4's large airframe and outstanding performance made it an excellent choice for a tactical reconnaissance aircraft. Almost concurrent with its order for the initial production of F-4Cs, the Air Force also issued SOR 196 which specified the requirements for the RF-4C. Initially designed to carry photographic, infrared, and laser systems, some RF-4Cs would later also employ an electronic reconnaissance system as well. This variant also retained the capability to deliver tactical nuclear weapons.

The initial prototype of the RF-4C flew for the first time on 8 August, 1963, and the first production aircraft made its maiden flight on 18 May, 1964. It entered operational service the following September and was deployed to SEA by the end of the year. Throughout the war, RF-4Cs provided invaluable reconnaissance of some of the most heavily defended targets in the history of warfare.

As aircraft become older, it takes more time and costs more money to maintain and operate them. But the Air Force never developed a replacement for the RF-4C. As a result, this version of the Phantom remained operational for over thirty years, the longest of any Phantom variant. The RF-4C and F-4E were only versions of the Phantom to serve in both the war in Vietnam and in Operations Desert Shield and Desert Storm. Some of the F-4G Wild Weasel aircraft that flew missions in Desert

Storm also saw combat in Vietnam, they were in their former F-4E configuration in SEA.

Just because an airframe is old does not mean that it cannot be operated effectively and with a high degree of reliability. During Operation Desert Shield, the 106th TRS of the Alabama ANG was tasked to fly 570 missions to take photographs of Iraqi installations and troop movements along the Saudi Arabian borders with Kuwait and Iraq. The unit maintained a one-hundred percent mission capable rate by flying all 570 missions. Replacement crews from the 192nd TRS of the Nevada ANG then flew 412 more missions. One RF-4C was lost in a non-combat related accident during Desert Shield, and another was destroyed in an accident after Desert Storm was over, but none were lost to enemy action. In addition to the Air National Guard aircraft, RF-4Cs from the 12th TRS of the 67th TRW and the 38th TRS of the 26th TRW also participated in the Gulf War. More information about the RF-4C can be found beginning on page 54.

The F-4C, F-4D, and RF-4C were the first Phantom variants acquired by the Air Force. Later the F-4E and the F-4G would also enter the Air Force inventory and write significant chapters in the history of military aviation. The story of the F-4E and F-4G can be found in Detail & Scale Volume 7, but starting on the following page is the most detailed look ever published of the Air Force's first three Phantom variants.

An RF-4C from the Nevada Air National Guard flies over California during the reconnaissance meet named "Photo Finish '85." The aircraft is painted in the European 1 camouflage scheme and has the unit's nickname "High Roller's" painted on the white fin cap. *(Official USAF photo)*

F-4C

To maximize the Phantom's capabilities to attack ground targets, the Air Force quickly began testing air-to-ground missiles on the aircraft. An early production F-4C is shown here with two AGM-12 Bullpup missiles on its inboard pylons. Notice that these pylons are the Navy type with the straight leading edge. Later, these would be replaced with pylons that had a curved leading edge on all Air Force Phantoms except the RF-4C. Also note that there is a launch rail on the pylon, and that the missile is attached to this rail rather than directly to the pylon. (National Archives)

Being the first fighter version of the Phantom acquired by the U. S. Air Force, the F-4C had relatively few major changes from the Navy's F-4B. To a considerable extent, this was due to then Secretary of Defense Robert McNamara's preoccupation with "commonality." Except for the Air Force markings that were painted on the aircraft, the main external difference that indicated that the Phantom was an F-4C was the change made to the main landing gear. The thin 7.7-inch high pressure tires used by the Navy on the F-4B were replaced with wider 11.5-inch tires. The main gear wheels were also wider and had anti-skid brakes. This change was necessitated by the fact that the Air Force aircraft would be used exclusively from land bases where long rollouts after landings would be the norm. In order for these wider wheels and tires to fit into the wings, bulges had to be added to the top and bottom wing panels and to the landing gear doors. Details of the main landing gear are illustrated on pages 23 and 24.

Internally there were other changes. Because the Air Force wanted the Phantom to be a fighter-bomber, a limited ground attack capability was added with appropriate avionics. An AN/AJB-7 nuclear bombing system was incorporated, and the AN/APQ-100 radar replaced the AN/APQ-72 used in the F-4B. The Navy's in-flight refueling probe was eliminated from the forward right side of the fuselage, and a receptacle for the high-speed boom system was added to the spine of the aircraft. The J79-GE-15 engine replaced the -8 version used with the F-4B. The -15 featured a cartridge self-starting system so that the F-4C could be used on airfields where there were no ground-based starter units available. Flight controls and side consoles were added to the rear cockpit, and the Air Force assigned this redesigned office to a rated pilot who served as the weapon systems officer. Usually called a

"wizzo" or "wuu-soo," as derived from the abbreviation WSO, the term GIB was also used to refer to the "guy in back."

For air-to-air combat, the Air Force initially supplemented the AIM-7 Sparrows with infrared AIM-4D Falcons instead of the Navy's AIM-9 Sidewinders. However, combat experience with the Falcons in Vietnam would later demonstrate that the missile was far less than satisfactory, so the Air Force changed to the more reliable Sidewinder.

Once it was decided what changes were to be incorporated into the F-4C, the Navy issued contracts to McDonnell on behalf of the Air Force for the production of the airframe. This occurred in March 1962. Meanwhile, the Air Force issued its own contracts for the J79-GE-15 engines. In April 1962, the mock-up of the F-4C was inspected, and production commenced.

The first flight of a production F-4C took place on 27 May, 1963, from St. Louis, and since the airframe was changed very little from the Navy's F-4B, there was no need to be overly cautious. As a result, Mach 2 was exceeded on this maiden flight. More importantly, the use of an airframe which was already tested and in service meant that immediate delivery to Air Force units could begin.

The first unit to receive the production F-4Cs was the 4453rd Combat Crew Training Wing at MacDill AFB. This unit had been flying the "borrowed" Navy F-4Bs, and had accumulated an impressive total of flying hours in the Phantom while awaiting their F-4Cs. Pilots of the 4453rd CCTW formed the cadre that began to train the first Air Force crews to check out in the Phantom. In January 1964, the 12th TFW, also based at MacDill, became the first combat unit to receive the F-4C, and it was declared

Loaded with Mk 82 Snakeye bombs on its inboard pylons, and LAU-10 5-inch rocket pods on the outboard stations, this F-4C is being readied for a strike in South Vietnam. Note that the rocket pods are fitted on multiple ejector racks on the outboard wing pylons, and that the MERs and pylons are attached at an angle to provide extra clearance between the ordnance and the landing gear. While this does not appear important with the rocket pods, other ordnance required that the anti-sway braces be adjusted to this slanted angle to provide even a minimal clearance. *(National Archives)*

operational with the aircraft in October 1964.

By the end of 1964, one squadron of F-4Cs had relocated to the far east, and early the following year F-4Cs were flying combat missions in Vietnam. On 10 July, 1965, two F-4Cs shot down two MiG-17s to score the aircraft's first air-to-air victories. Throughout the rest of 1965 and during 1966, the number of F-4Cs deployed to SEA continued to rise, but so did the losses. By the end of 1966, a total of fifty-four F-4Cs had been lost in combat.

Production continued until 4 May, 1966, during which time 583 F-4Cs were produced. Although none were built for export, thirty-six former USAF F-4Cs were transferred to Spain beginning in 1971. They were redesignated C-12s by the Spanish Air Force.

In 1968, during the war in Vietnam, thirty-six F-4Cs were converted to EF-4Cs for use in the dangerous air defense suppression mission. These temporary Wild Weasel IV Phantoms were fitted with additional radar warning sensors to include antennas associated with the AN/APR-25 radar homing and warning (RHAW) system. These were located in the fairing under the radome and on the cover for the parabrake compartment. The AN/APR-26 SAM launch warning system was also fitted, and its small, omni-directional antenna was located just aft of the radome at the bottom of the nose section. More noticeable were the triangular antennas of the ER-142 homing system which were located high on the sides of the nose, just forward of and below the windscreen. The APR-26

was subsequently replaced with the APR-46, and the ALR-53 supplanted the ER-142.

EF-4Cs were usually armed with the AGM-45 Shrike anti-radiation missile, but other conventional ordnance was also used for the SAM suppression mission. However, the EF-4C was not capable of employing the AGM-78 Standard ARM, which was used by the F-105G in Vietnam and after the war by the F-4G Wild Weasel aircraft. This proved to be a limitation of some magnitude, because the Shrike was a first-generation anti-radiation missile with capabilities that were considerably less than the Standard ARM.

The 67th TFS of the 18th TFW received their EF-4C at their home base of Kadena AB, Okinawa, but they flew their combat missions out of Thailand. Other EF-4Cs were deployed to Europe and were assigned to the 81st TFS of the 52nd TFW at Spangdahlem AB, Germany. The EF-4Cs were returned to their original F-4C configuration before being turned over to units of the Air National Guard.

In 1972, ten F-4Cs were transferred to the 170th TFS of the Illinois Air National Guard. In 1976 the 199th TFS of the Hawaii ANG received F-4Cs, and this unit was followed by by others between 1978 and 1984. A total of fourteen Guard squadrons operated the F-4C until the last aircraft was retired in 1989. The 93rd TFS was the only Air Force Reserve squadron to fly this version of the Phantom. It was equipped with F-4Cs from 1978 until 1983 when it upgraded to F-4Ds.

F-4C, 64-840, was one of thirty-six aircraft converted to the EF-4C Wild Weasel sub-variant. It is shown here armed with two AGM-45 Shrike anti-radiation missiles. Note the ER-142 antenna just forward of and slightly below the canopy. The ZG tail code indicates that the aircraft was assigned to the 67th TFS of the 18th TFW when this photograph was taken in 1972. *(Rotramel collection)*

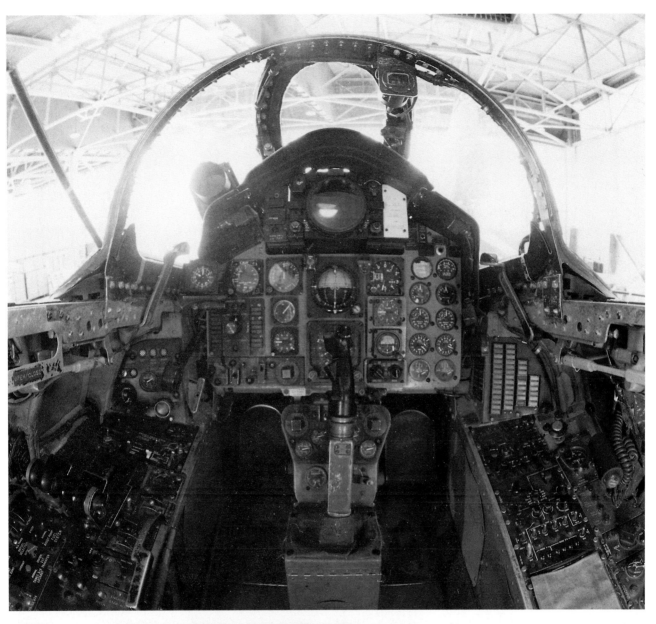

Above: This wide angle photograph shows the details of the front cockpit in an F-4C. (McDonnell Douglas)

Left: The instrument panel and radar scope in the rear cockpit of an F-4C can be seen in this view. Some strategically located pieces of paper cover some classified items of equipment associated with the radar homing and warning system.

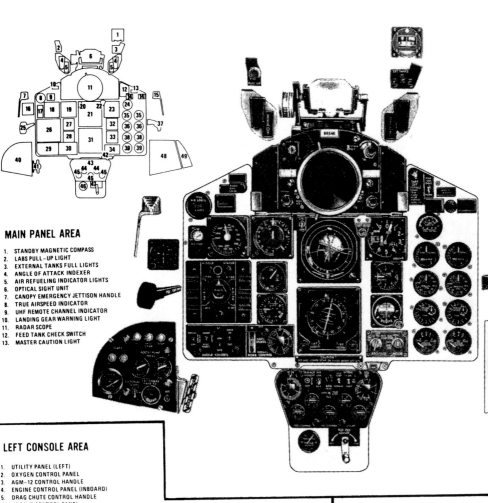

14. FIRE-OVERHEAT WARNING LIGHTS
15. CANOPY MANUAL UNLOCK HANDLE
16. EIGHT DAY CLOCK
17. FLIGHT INSTRUMENT LIGHTS
    CONTROL PANEL
18. RADAR ALTIMETER
19. AIRSPEED AND MACH INDICATOR
20. REFERENCE SYSTEM SELECTOR SWITCH
21. ALTITUDE DIRECTOR INDICATOR (ADI)
22. MARKER BEACON LIGHT
23. ALTIMETER
24. INTERNAL FUEL QUANTITY INDICATOR
25. LANDING GEAR CONTROL HANDLE

26. MISSILE STATUS PANEL
27. ANGLE OF ATTACK INDICATOR
28. ACCELEROMETER
29. MISSILE CONTROL PANEL
30. BOMB CONTROL PANEL
31. HORIZONTAL SITUATION INDICATOR (HSI)
32. VERTICAL VELOCITY INDICATOR
33. EMERGENCY ATTITUDE INDICATOR
34. NAVIGATION FUNCTION SELECTOR PANEL
35. FUEL FLOW INDICATORS
36. TACHOMETERS
37. ARRESTING HOOK CONTROL HANDLE
38. EXHAUST GAS TEMPERATURE INDICATORS

MAIN PANEL AREA

1. STANDBY MAGNETIC COMPASS
2. LABS PULL-UP LIGHT
3. EXTERNAL TANKS FULL LIGHTS
4. ANGLE OF ATTACK INDEXER
5. AIR REFUELING INDICATOR LIGHTS
6. OPTICAL SIGHT UNIT
7. CANOPY EMERGENCY JETTISON HANDLE
8. TRUE AIRSPEED INDICATOR
9. UHF REMOTE CHANNEL INDICATOR
10. LANDING GEAR WARNING LIGHT
11. RADAR SCOPE
12. FEED TANK CHECK SWITCH
13. MASTER CAUTION LIGHT

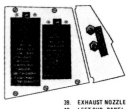

39. EXHAUST NOZZLE POSITION INDICATORS
40. LEFT SUB-PANEL
41. EMERGENCY BRAKE CONTROL HANDLE
42. VOR MODE LIGHT
43. MULTIPLE WEAPONS CONTROL PANEL
44. OIL PRESSURE INDICATORS
45. HYDRAULIC PRESSURE INDICATORS
46. PNEUMATIC PRESSURE INDICATORS
47. RUDDER PEDAL ADJUSTMENT CRANK
48. RIGHT SUB-PANEL (TELELIGHTS)
49. INSTRUMENT LIGHTS INTENSITY
    CIRCUIT BREAKERS

LEFT CONSOLE AREA

1. UTILITY PANEL (LEFT)
2. OXYGEN CONTROL PANEL
3. AGM-12 CONTROL HANDLE
4. ENGINE CONTROL PANEL (INBOARD)
5. DRAG CHUTE CONTROL HANDLE
6. VOR/ILS CONTROL PANEL
7. AUTOMATIC FLIGHT CONTROL SYSTEM
   CONTROL PANEL
8. BOARDING STEPS POSITION INDICATOR
9. INTERCOM SYSTEM CONTROL PANEL
10. BLANK PANEL
11. BLANK PANEL
12. ARMAMENT SAFETY OVERRIDE SWITCH
13. ANTI-G SUIT CONTROL VALVE
14. OUTBOARD PYLON JETTISON SELECT
    SWITCH
15. AUXILIARY ARMAMENT CONTROL PANEL
16. FUEL CONTROL PANEL
17. RAM AIR TURBINE CONTROL HANDLE
18. EXTRA PICTURE SWITCH
19. CANOPY SELECTOR
20. FLAP CONTROL PANEL
21. EJECT LIGHT/SWITCH
22. ENGINE CONTROL PANEL (OUTBOARD)
23. THROTTLES

RIGHT CONSOLE AREA

1. CNI EQUIPMENT COOLING RESET BUTTON
2. EMERGENCY VENT HANDLE
3. UTILITY PANEL (RIGHT)
4. DEFOG/FOOT HEAT CONTROL PANEL
5. CIRCUIT BREAKER PANEL
6. TEMPERATURE CONTROL PANEL
7. EMERGENCY FLOODLIGHTS PANEL
8. COCKPIT LIGHTS CONTROL PANEL
9. STANDBY ATTITUDE CIRCUIT BREAKER AND
   INTENSITY CONTROL PANEL
10. INSTRUMENT LIGHTS INTENSITY
    CONTROL PANEL
11. EXTERIOR LIGHTS CONTROL PANEL
12. UTILITY ELECTRICAL RECEPTACLE
13. BLANK PANEL
14. COMPASS CONTROL PANEL
15. CLUSTER BOMB UNIT CONTROL PANEL
16. DCU-94A BOMB CONTROL—MONITOR PANEL
17. IFF CONTROL PANEL
18. NAVIGATION CONTROL PANEL
19. COMMUNICATION CONTROL PANEL
20. GENERATOR CONTROL PANEL

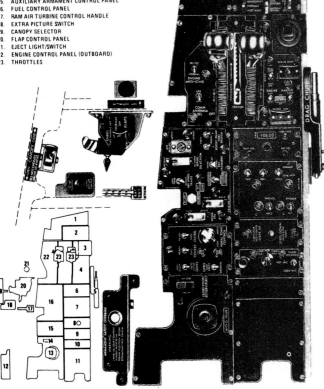

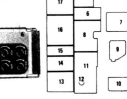

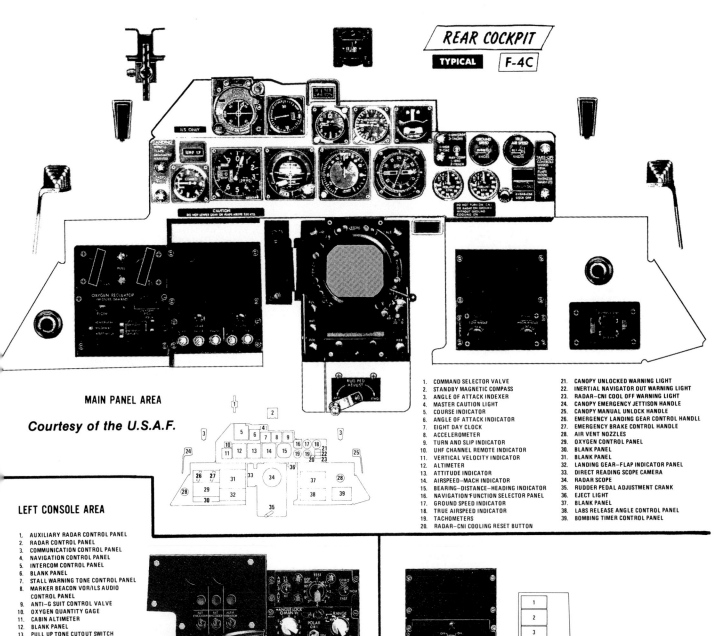

ILS ONLY

CAUTION
DO NOT LOWER GEAR OR FLAPS ABOVE 250 KTS.

MAIN PANEL AREA

Courtesy of the U.S.A.F.

1. COMMAND SELECTOR VALVE	21. CANOPY UNLOCKED WARNING LIGHT
2. STANDBY MAGNETIC COMPASS	22. INERTIAL NAVIGATOR OUT WARNING LIGHT
3. ANGLE OF ATTACK INDEXER	23. RADAR–CNI COOL OFF WARNING LIGHT
4. MASTER CAUTION LIGHT	24. CANOPY EMERGENCY JETTISON HANDLE
5. COURSE INDICATOR	25. CANOPY MANUAL UNLOCK HANDLE
6. ANGLE OF ATTACK INDICATOR	26. EMERGENCY LANDING GEAR CONTROL HANDLE
7. EIGHT DAY CLOCK	27. EMERGENCY BRAKE CONTROL HANDLE
8. ACCELEROMETER	28. AIR VENT NOZZLES
9. TURN AND SLIP INDICATOR	29. OXYGEN CONTROL PANEL
10. UHF CHANNEL REMOTE INDICATOR	30. BLANK PANEL
11. VERTICAL VELOCITY INDICATOR	31. BLANK PANEL
12. ALTIMETER	32. LANDING GEAR–FLAP INDICATOR PANEL
13. ATTITUDE INDICATOR	33. DIRECT READING SCOPE CAMERA
14. AIRSPEED–MACH INDICATOR	34. RADAR SCOPE
15. BEARING–DISTANCE–HEADING INDICATOR	35. RUDDER PEDAL ADJUSTMENT CRANK
16. NAVIGATION FUNCTION SELECTOR PANEL	36. EJECT LIGHT
17. GROUND SPEED INDICATOR	37. BLANK PANEL
18. TRUE AIRSPEED INDICATOR	38. LABS RELEASE ANGLE CONTROL PANEL
19. TACHOMETERS	39. BOMBING TIMER CONTROL PANEL
20. RADAR–CNI COOLING RESET BUTTON	

LEFT CONSOLE AREA

1. AUXILIARY RADAR CONTROL PANEL
2. RADAR CONTROL PANEL
3. COMMUNICATION CONTROL PANEL
4. NAVIGATION CONTROL PANEL
5. INTERCOM CONTROL PANEL
6. BLANK PANEL
7. STALL WARNING TONE CONTROL PANEL
8. MARKER BEACON VOR/ILS AUDIO
   CONTROL PANEL
9. ANTI-G SUIT CONTROL VALVE
10. OXYGEN QUANTITY GAGE
11. CABIN ALTIMETER
12. BLANK PANEL
13. PULL UP TONE CUTOUT SWITCH
14. EMERGENCY FLAP CONTROL PANEL
15. CANOPY SELECTOR
16. THROTTLES
17. BLANK PANEL
18. CIRCUIT BREAKER PANEL NO. 5

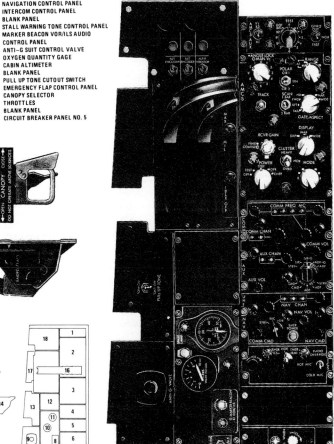

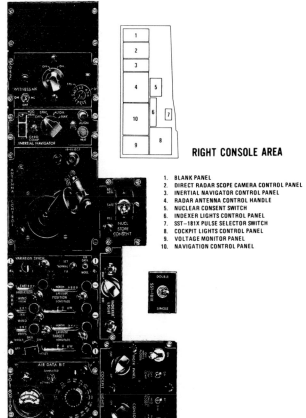

RIGHT CONSOLE AREA

1. BLANK PANEL
2. DIRECT RADAR SCOPE CAMERA CONTROL PANEL
3. INERTIAL NAVIGATOR CONTROL PANEL
4. RADAR ANTENNA CONTROL HANDLE
5. NUCLEAR CONSENT SWITCH
6. INDEXER LIGHTS CONTROL PANEL
7. SST–181X PULSE SELECTOR SWITCH
8. COCKPIT LIGHTS CONTROL PANEL
9. VOLTAGE MONITOR PANEL
10. NAVIGATION CONTROL PANEL

F-4D

The F-4D could usually be distinguished from the earlier F-4C by the "bump" on the infrared sensor beneath the radome. This particular aircraft belonged to the 4485th Test Squadron of the Tactical Air Weapons Center which was based at Eglin Air Force Base, Florida. An ALQ-101 ECM pod is attached to the right inboard pylon. **(National Archives)**

The F-4C was a better fighter-bomber than the F-105, and in some important respects it offered better performance in the air-to-air arena than did the F-106. However, the Air Force realized that the Phantom's airframe offered a far greater potential than provided by the F-4C. A considerable number of proposals were studied, some of which offered little improvement over the F-4C, while others promised a significant increase in the capabilities of the aircraft. Even the addition of an internal 20mm Vulcan cannon was considered, but the lessons of Vietnam had not yet been learned, and this feature was not included. It would reappear later in the F-4E. What the Air Force did decide on was a new Phantom variant with improvements in both the air-to-air and air-to-ground capabilities.

With the prospects of war in Vietnam growing more likely every day, the Air Force had the Navy issue a letter contract for the F-4D in March 1964, even before the first combat wing of F-4Cs became operationally ready. The first prototype made its initial flight in June 1965, and the first production aircraft flew the following December. Deliveries began in April 1966, and production continued until February 1968, when the number of F-4Ds built for the U. S. Air Force reached 793. Additionally, thirty-two F-4Ds were built for Iran, bringing the total production to 825.

Externally, there was very little physical difference between the F-4C and the F-4D. The one quick way to distinguish the two was to look at the fairing beneath the radome. Although missing from some early F-4Ds, this fairing was soon added and had a noticeable hump on its underside. By contrast, the fairing on the F-4C had a smoothly curved underside like that used on the previous F-4B. But on the F-4D, the pre-amplifier and antennas for the AN/APR-25/-26 were carried inside the fairing, and the hump was simply an enlargement to accommodate these pieces of equipment. Late in the service life of the F-4D, the shape of this hump was changed again, and the small nodes associated with the AN/ALR-69(V)-2 radar homing and warning (RHAW) system replaced the earlier equipment. Photographs of the different fairings can be found on page 25. The AN/APS-107A RHAW system was also installed, and its antenna was located in a fairing at the top of the trailing edge of the vertical tail.

The AN/APQ-109A radar replaced the APQ-100 used in the F-4C. At first glance, the two radars looked almost identical, but the APQ-109A was both smaller and lighter. (Photographs of both radars can be found on page 37.) It was part of the AN/APA-165 radar set group which provided air-to-ground ranging capability. The AN/ASQ-91 weapons release system greatly improved the delivery of air-to-ground weapons. Some F-4Ds became the first fighters to use of "smart" weapons in the form of laser guided bombs. Later, some others were also equipped to employ electro-optical weapons like the GBU-8 bomb and the AGM-65 Maverick missile. The F-4D also retained the AN/AJB-7 all-altitude bombing system which permitted the delivery of nuclear weapons.

To improve performance in air-to-air combat, the AN/ASG-22 lead computing gunsight was added. The gyro and amplifier for this sight were located behind the rear cockpit, and this required that the Number 1 fuel cell be reduced in size. This resulted in a reduction of eighty-

A total of twelve Mk 82, 500-pound bombs are shown loaded on this F-4D. Three are on triple ejector racks (TER) which are attached to each inboard pylon, and six are on the multiple ejector rack (MER) on the centerline station. Also note the ALQ-71 ECM pod in the forward right Sparrow bay and the combat camera under the right intake just below where the leading edge of the wing meets the fuselage.
(National Archives)

three gallons of internal fuel. Sharing this space with the gyro and amplifier were the AN/ASQ-91 weapons release computer and the AN/ASN-63 internal navigation system. As with the F-4C, it was originally planned that the F-4D would use the AIM-4D Falcon infrared homing missile along with its AIM-7 Sparrows, but the AIM-4Ds were later replaced with AIM-9 Sidewinders after the Falcons proved unreliable.

There were a number of systems fitted only to a limited number of F-4Ds. Among the most important of these was the AN/ALR-92 LORAN precision navigation system with its characteristic "towel rack" antenna which was located on the spine of the aircraft. Twelve aircraft were modified to carry the Pave Knife pod on one of the inboard pylons, and this became the one of the first designators used with laser guided bombs. The smaller Pave Spike pod could be carried in a forward Sparrow missile bay, and a considerable number of F-4Ds were equipped to carry this pod. Although any F-4D could carry and drop the laser guided bombs, only those specially equipped to employ the pods could designate the target. Photographs of both pods can be found on page 53.

A total of 194 F-4Ds was lost during the war in Vietnam. This figure means that nearly twenty-five per-cent of the 793 F-4Ds built for the U. S. Air Force did not return home from the war. Of this total, 170 were lost to hostile action, while the remaining twenty-four were destroyed in non-combat accidents. Only seventeen of the

170 combat losses were a result of air-to-air action, while the F-4D was credited with shooting down 44.5 enemy aircraft. Although this is the highest total for any Phantom variant, it works out to only a 2.6-to-1 kill ratio. Three out of every four F-4Ds lost in combat were shot down by anti-aircraft artillery (AAA), while surface-to-air missiles (SAM) were credited with only six percent of the losses.

The Air Force explored the possibility of converting F-4Ds to EF-4D Wild Weasel aircraft incorporating the AN/APR-38 advanced avionics system and the AGM-78 Standard anti-radiation missile. Four aircraft were actually modified for evaluation purposes, and the first made its initial flight on 27 November, 1972. Although ninety F-4Ds were scheduled to become EF-4Ds, no further conversions were made, nor was there any production of this variant. Instead, the program was changed, and F-4Es were modified to the F-4G Wild Weasel version.

Beginning in 1977, many F-4Ds were turned over to the Air National Guard, while Air Force Reserve squadrons began to receive this Phantom variant in 1980. Five Reserve and fourteen Air National Guard squadrons flew F-4Ds until they were finally replaced by newer aircraft. The last F-4Ds were retired from the Reserve and the Guard in 1990. In addition to the thirty-two F-4Ds which were produced for Iran, the Air Force transferred approximately sixty aircraft from its inventory to the Republic of Korea.

Two GBU-10 laser guided bombs are attached to the inboard pylons of this F-4D. The FG tail code indicates that the aircraft was assigned to the 433rd TFS of the 8th TFW. The aircraft is shown as its pilot carefully taxied out of the protective revetment for a mission over North Vietnam. It is noteworthy that two Mk 82, 500-pound bombs can also be seen attached to a MER on the centerline station.
(National Archives)

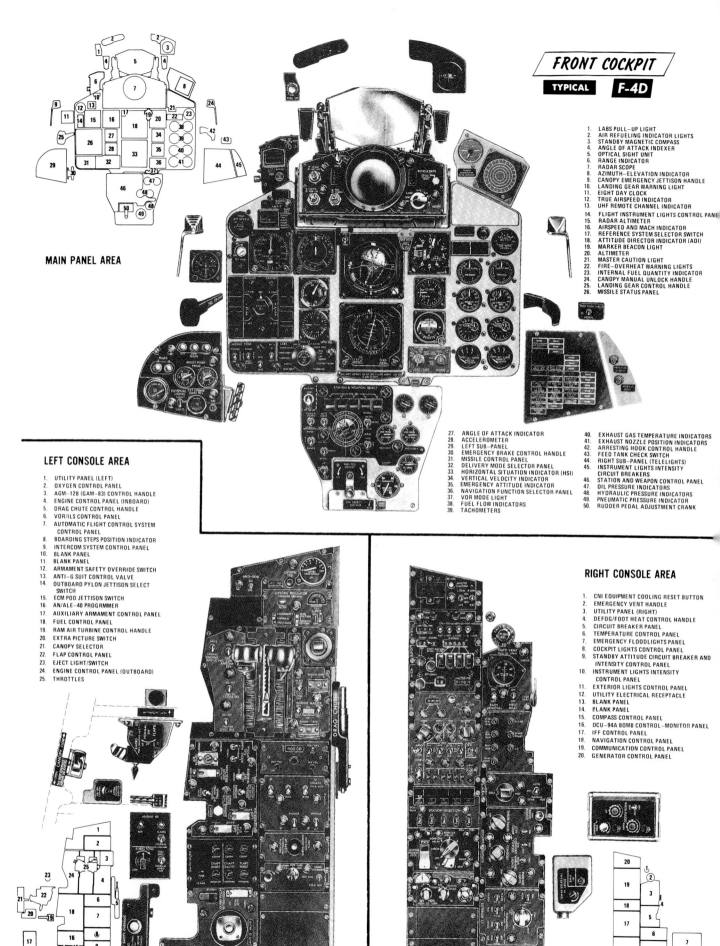

MAIN PANEL AREA

1. LABS PULL–UP LIGHT
2. AIR REFUELING INDICATOR LIGHTS
3. STANDBY MAGNETIC COMPASS
4. ANGLE OF ATTACK INDEXER
5. OPTICAL SIGHT UNIT
6. RANGE INDICATOR
7. RADAR SCOPE
8. AZIMUTH–ELEVATION INDICATOR
9. CANOPY EMERGENCY JETTISON HANDLE
10. LANDING GEAR WARNING LIGHT
11. EIGHT DAY CLOCK
12. TRUE AIRSPEED INDICATOR
13. UHF REMOTE CHANNEL INDICATOR
14. FLIGHT INSTRUMENT LIGHTS CONTROL PANEL
15. RADAR ALTIMETER
16. AIRSPEED AND MACH INDICATOR
17. REFERENCE SYSTEM SELECTOR SWITCH
18. ATTITUDE DIRECTOR INDICATOR (ADI)
19. MARKER BEACON LIGHT
20. ALTIMETER
21. MASTER CAUTION LIGHT
22. FIRE–OVERHEAT WARNING LIGHTS
23. INTERNAL FUEL QUANTITY INDICATOR
24. CANOPY MANUAL UNLOCK HANDLE
25. LANDING GEAR CONTROL HANDLE
26. MISSILE STATUS PANEL

27. ANGLE OF ATTACK INDICATOR
28. ACCELEROMETER
29. LEFT SUB–PANEL
30. EMERGENCY BRAKE CONTROL HANDLE
31. MISSILE CONTROL PANEL
32. DELIVERY MODE SELECTOR PANEL
33. HORIZONTAL SITUATION INDICATOR (HSI)
34. VERTICAL VELOCITY INDICATOR
35. EMERGENCY ATTITUDE INDICATOR
36. NAVIGATION FUNCTION SELECTOR PANEL
37. VOR MODE LIGHT
38. FUEL FLOW INDICATORS
39. TACHOMETERS

40. EXHAUST GAS TEMPERATURE INDICATORS
41. EXHAUST NOZZLE POSITION INDICATORS
42. ARRESTING HOOK CONTROL HANDLE
43. FEED TANK CHECK SWITCH
44. RIGHT SUB–PANEL (TELELIGHTS)
45. INSTRUMENT LIGHTS INTENSITY CIRCUIT BREAKERS
46. STATION AND WEAPON CONTROL PANEL
47. OIL PRESSURE INDICATORS
48. HYDRAULIC PRESSURE INDICATORS
49. PNEUMATIC PRESSURE INDICATOR
50. RUDDER PEDAL ADJUSTMENT CRANK

LEFT CONSOLE AREA

1. UTILITY PANEL (LEFT)
2. OXYGEN CONTROL PANEL
3. AGM–12B (GAM–83) CONTROL HANDLE
4. ENGINE CONTROL PANEL (INBOARD)
5. DRAG CHUTE CONTROL HANDLE
6. VOR/ILS CONTROL PANEL
7. AUTOMATIC FLIGHT CONTROL SYSTEM CONTROL PANEL
8. BOARDING STEPS POSITION INDICATOR
9. INTERCOM SYSTEM CONTROL PANEL
10. BLANK PANEL
11. BLANK PANEL
12. ARMAMENT SAFETY OVERRIDE SWITCH
13. ANTI–G SUIT CONTROL VALVE
14. OUTBOARD PYLON JETTISON SELECT SWITCH
15. ECM POD JETTISON SWITCH
16. AN/ALE–40 PROGRMMER
17. AUXILIARY ARMAMENT CONTROL PANEL
18. FUEL CONTROL PANEL
19. RAM AIR TURBINE CONTROL HANDLE
20. EXTRA PICTURE SWITCH
21. CANOPY SELECTOR
22. FLAP CONTROL PANEL
23. EJECT LIGHT/SWITCH
24. ENGINE CONTROL PANEL (OUTBOARD)
25. THROTTLES

RIGHT CONSOLE AREA

1. CNI EQUIPMENT COOLING RESET BUTTON
2. EMERGENCY VENT HANDLE
3. UTILITY PANEL (RIGHT)
4. DEFOG/FOOT HEAT CONTROL HANDLE
5. CIRCUIT BREAKER PANEL
6. TEMPERATURE CONTROL PANEL
7. EMERGENCY FLOODLIGHTS PANEL
8. COCKPIT LIGHTS CONTROL PANEL
9. STANDBY ATTITUDE CIRCUIT BREAKER AND INTENSITY CONTROL PANEL
10. INSTRUMENT LIGHTS INTENSITY CONTROL PANEL
11. EXTERIOR LIGHTS CONTROL PANEL
12. UTILITY ELECTRICAL RECEPTACLE
13. BLANK PANEL
14. PLANK PANEL
15. COMPASS CONTROL PANEL
16. DCU–94A BOMB CONTROL–MONITOR PANEL
17. IFF CONTROL PANEL
18. NAVIGATION CONTROL PANEL
19. COMMUNICATION CONTROL PANEL
20. GENERATOR CONTROL PANEL

Courtesy of the U.S.A.F.

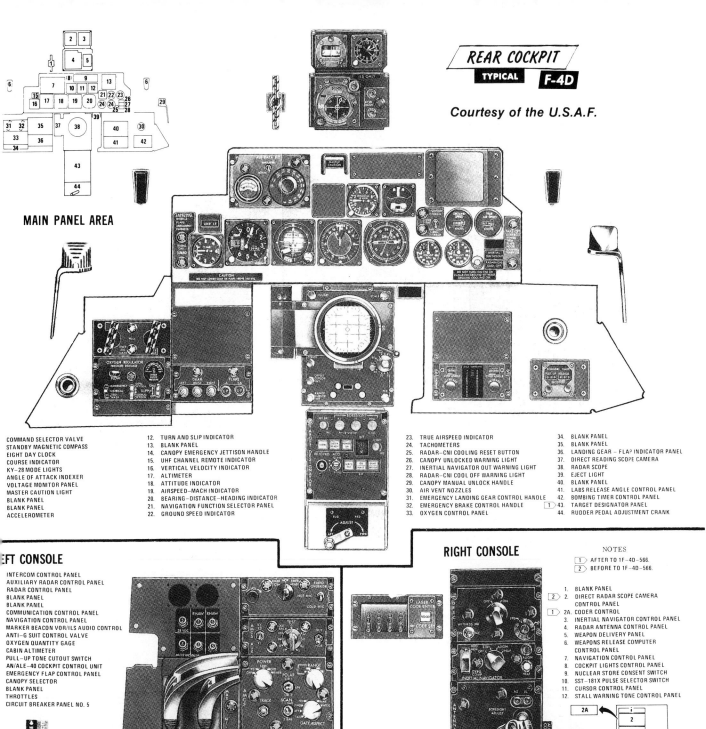

MAIN PANEL AREA

COMMAND SELECTOR VALVE	12. TURN AND SLIP INDICATOR
STANDBY MAGNETIC COMPASS	13. BLANK PANEL
EIGHT DAY CLOCK	14. CANOPY EMERGENCY JETTISON HANDLE
COURSE INDICATOR	15. UHF CHANNEL REMOTE INDICATOR
KY-28 MODE LIGHTS	16. VERTICAL VELOCITY INDICATOR
ANGLE OF ATTACK INDEXER	17. ALTIMETER
VOLTAGE MONITOR PANEL	18. ATTITUDE INDICATOR
MASTER CAUTION LIGHT	19. AIRSPEED–MACH INDICATOR
BLANK PANEL	20. BEARING–DISTANCE–HEADING INDICATOR
BLANK PANEL	21. NAVIGATION FUNCTION SELECTOR PANEL
ACCELEROMETER	22. GROUND SPEED INDICATOR

23. TRUE AIRSPEED INDICATOR	34. BLANK PANEL
24. TACHOMETERS	35. BLANK PANEL
25. RADAR–CNI COOLING RESET BUTTON	36. LANDING GEAR – FLAP INDICATOR PANEL
26. CANOPY UNLOCKED WARNING LIGHT	37. DIRECT READING SCOPE CAMERA
27. INERTIAL NAVIGATOR OUT WARNING LIGHT	38. RADAR SCOPE
28. RADAR–CNI COOL OFF WARNING LIGHT	39. EJECT LIGHT
29. CANOPY MANUAL UNLOCK HANDLE	40. BLANK PANEL
30. AIR VENT NOZZLES	41. LABS RELEASE ANGLE CONTROL PANEL
31. EMERGENCY LANDING GEAR CONTROL HANDLE	42. BOMBING TIMER CONTROL PANEL
32. EMERGENCY BRAKE CONTROL HANDLE [1]	43. TARGET DESIGNATOR PANEL
33. OXYGEN CONTROL PANEL	44. RUDDER PEDAL ADJUSTMENT CRANK

LEFT CONSOLE

INTERCOM CONTROL PANEL
AUXILIARY RADAR CONTROL PANEL
RADAR CONTROL PANEL
BLANK PANEL
BLANK PANEL
COMMUNICATION CONTROL PANEL
NAVIGATION CONTROL PANEL
MARKER BEACON VOR/ILS AUDIO CONTROL
ANTI-G SUIT CONTROL VALVE
OXYGEN QUANTITY GAGE
CABIN ALTIMETER
PULL-UP TONE CUTOUT SWITCH
AN/ALE-40 COCKPIT CONTROL UNIT
EMERGENCY FLAP CONTROL PANEL
CANOPY SELECTOR
BLANK PANEL
THROTTLES
CIRCUIT BREAKER PANEL NO. 5

RIGHT CONSOLE

NOTES

[1] AFTER TO 1F-4D-566.
[2] BEFORE TO 1F-4D-566.

1. BLANK PANEL
[2] 2. DIRECT RADAR SCOPE CAMERA
    CONTROL PANEL
[1] 2A. CODER CONTROL
3. INERTIAL NAVIGATOR CONTROL PANEL
4. RADAR ANTENNA CONTROL PANEL
5. WEAPON DELIVERY PANEL
6. WEAPONS RELEASE COMPUTER
    CONTROL PANEL
7. NAVIGATION CONTROL PANEL
8. COCKPIT LIGHTS CONTROL PANEL
9. NUCLEAR STORE CONSENT SWITCH
10. SST-181X PULSE SELECTOR SWITCH
11. CURSOR CONTROL PANEL
12. STALL WARNING TONE CONTROL PANEL

17

F-4C, F-4D, & RF-4C DETAILS

ENGINE DETAILS

The F-4C, F-4D, and RF-4C were all powered by two General Electric J79-GE-15 engines, each capable of producing 17,000 pounds of thrust in afterburner at 7,685 rpm. At the same rpm, but without the afterburner operating, thrust was 10,900 pounds. Normal power produced 10,300 pounds at 7,385 rpm. The J79-GE-15 was 208.45 inches long with its afterburner and had a maximum diameter of 38.3 inches. Its dry weight was 3,627 pounds. This version of the J79 was characterized by a shorter variable position ejector nozzle or eyelid as compared to later versions of the engine used on subsequent Phantom variants. The two photographs at right show left and right side views of a complete J79-GE-15 engine which has been removed from an RF-4C.

These views look down the Phantom's two large air inlets back to the forward end of the engines. The photograph at left was taken inside the right inlet, while the photograph at right shows the interior of the left inlet. Variable inlet geometry was used to control the air flow to the engines regardless of whether the aircraft was stationary on the ground or flying at twice the speed of sound. The speed of the air entering the inlets was measured by the probe located just inside each inlet on the outer wall. Based on the speed of the air that was entering the inlets, two movable ramps, located opposite the probe on the inside wall, were automatically positioned so as to create shock waves inside the inlet. These shock waves reduced the velocity of the air to a subsonic speed that could be used by the engines.

Above: The shorter ejector nozzle of the J79-GE-15 engine is illustrated in this photograph.

Right: With access panels opened, the underside details of an installed engine are visible in this view that looks aft from the forward end of the engine.

With the variable nozzles opened almost to the full open position, details of the aft end of the engines are visible here.

Actually taken inside the nozzle of one of the engines, this photograph provides a detailed look at the interior of the afterburner and the flame holder which is located at the forward end of the afterburner.

CANOPY DETAILS

Left and above: The standard windscreen with its framing is shown at left. This was common to all Phantom variants as produced. However, late in their operational life a few aircraft, including some RF-4Cs, were fitted with the frameless windscreen illustrated in the photograph above.

The area just behind the front seat is shown here. The hydraulic cylinder and piston for raising and lowering the forward canopy can be seen at the center of this photograph which was taken from the left side of the aircraft.

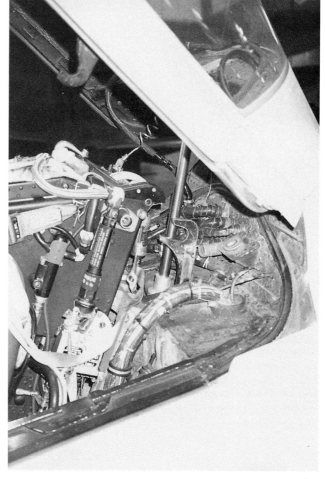

Also taken from the left side, this photograph shows the area behind the rear seat. Again the piston and cylinder that raises and lowers the rear canopy are visible.

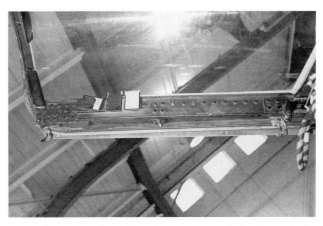

Details of the interior framing on the right side of the forward canopy are illustrated here. Notice the hook at each end that locks the canopy into the fuselage when it is in the closed position.

The cockpits were covered by two separate canopies, and the interior framework was painted flat black. This photograph shows the inside of the framing for the left side of the forward canopy.

The rear canopy is shown here. The inner framing on the left side is visible.

This photograph shows the details of the inside framework on the right side of the rear canopy.

LANDING GEAR DETAILS

NOSE LANDING GEAR

On the RF-4C, the lower UHF blade antenna was positioned below the lights on the forward nose gear door. Also note that the total temperature probe is also on the door just above and to the left of the taxi lights.

The landing gear used on the F-4C, F-4D, and RF-4C was the same except for some minor detail differences that pertained to the forward nose gear door. This photograph shows the forward nose gear door as used on the F-4C and F-4D. Note that the lower UHF blade antenna is located on the door above the two taxi lights. The total temperature probe is on the fuselage just below the left air conditioning scoop.

Details of the interior of the nose landing gear well are shown in this view that looks up, aft, and to the right in the well. The inside of the aft nose gear door is also visible. Wheel wells on most Phantoms were painted white. The nose gear was actuated by a hydraulic arm mounted to the right side of the well and strut.

Right and left side views of the nose gear reveal details of the strut and the wheels.

RIGHT MAIN LANDING GEAR

This front view of the right main landing gear provides a good look at the struts and the angle of the outer gear doors. Air Force Phantoms had wider main wheels and tires than did the F-4A, F-4B, F-4N, and some RF-4B variants used by the Navy and Marines. To accommodate the wider tires, bulges had to be added in the upper and lower wing panels as well as the main gear door that is attached to the strut. The bulge in the door is visible in this photograph.

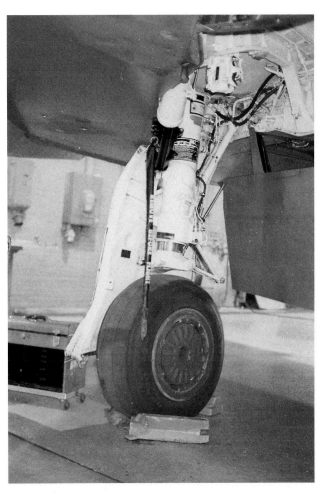

More details of the right main strut, wheel, and tire can be seen from this angle. Note that the hydraulic actuating arm has been secured with a clamp to keep it from accidently collapsing while the aircraft is on the ground. This clamp is painted red and has a REMOVE BEFORE FLIGHT streamer attached to it.

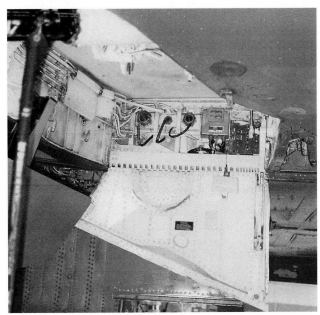

The inner right main gear door is shown here as is the inner portion of the right main gear well.

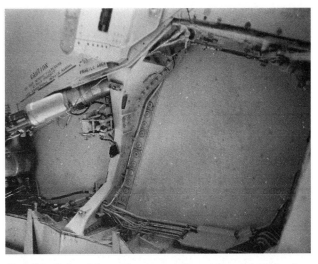

Details of the right main gear well are shown in this view that looks directly up into the well. The main strut is to the left of the photograph, and the aft end of the right inboard pylon can be seen at the top. It is evident that there is very little clearance between the gear door and the pylon.

LEFT MAIN LANDING GEAR

The left main landing gear is essentially a mirror image of the right. This photograph provides an excellent view of the right main gear strut, wheel, and tire. In this case, the speed brake just aft of the gear has been disconnected from its hydraulic actuator during maintenance and is hanging down much closer to the gear than it normally would. (See page 29.)

The inner left main gear door and its hydraulically actuated extension/retraction mechanism are shown here. The hydraulic lines running along the inner and aft sides of the well are also clearly illustrated.

A jacking position is located behind a small panel at the bottom of each main gear door. With the jack in place, maintenance personnel prepare to lift the gear in order to inspect the brakes. Again, note the bulges in the center main gear door.

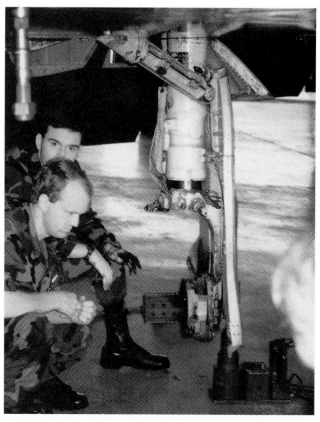

With the left main gear strut on a jack and the wheel removed, ground crew personnel inspect the gear during regularly scheduled maintenance.

FUSELAGE DETAILS

The Navy F-4B had a fairing under the radome which housed an AAA-4 infrared seeker. Most production F-4Cs also had the same fairing under the radome, however, the seeker was not installed.

Initially, F-4Ds were produced without the fairing under the radome. Although these were soon added, they were used for a different purpose. Instead of housing an infrared seeker, the new fairing, with its distinctive lower bulge, contained the preamplifier and antennas for the APR-25/26 radar homing and warning system. In most cases, the best way to visually distinguish an F-4C from an F-4D was to look at this faring under the radome. A smoothly curved fairing, as illustrated in the top photograph on this page, indicated an F-4C. The fairing with the lower hump, as seen in this picture, meant that the aircraft was an F-4D. (Cockle)

Late in the operational life of the F-4D, the AN/ALR-69(V)-2 RHAW system was added, and the antennas were located in the chin fairing which was modified once again. These two photographs show the six nodes on the fairing. Two are located at the forward end of the pod, and four are on the small mount at the bottom of the fairing. This configuration was sometimes called the "herpies mod."

All Phantoms had air conditioning scoops on each side of the nose. The scoops used on the F-4C and F-4D were the same as used on Navy Phantoms, and the left scoop on an F-4C is illustrated in this photograph. The air conditioning scoops on the RF-4C were considerably different as can be seen on page 56. Beneath the scoop is the total temperature probe and the lower TACAN antenna.

On the right side of the nose section is another formation light panel but no rescue apparatus. Some Phantoms had a black and yellow marking on this side indicating that the emergency rescue lanyard was located on the opposite side of the aircraft. The right air conditioning scoop is visible as is the location of a static vent on the radome. This vent is marked with a red circle, and white stencilling under the vent warns ground crew personnel not to plug or deform the vent. Another static vent is located in the same place on the opposite side of the radome. The marking, consisting of four dots and positioned just forward of the light panel, indicates the location of air conditioning equipment inside the aircraft. The marking on the aft nose gear door indicates the location of nitrogen.

At the center of the fuselage on each side was the middle formation light panel. The marking above it, which appears to have a shape similar to a question mark, indicates a hoist point. The upper TACAN antenna can be seen on the spine.

Details of the left side of the nose section are illustrated in this photo. Note the two steps with the spring loaded doors. Black lines extend from the steps up to the canopy rail. The location for the device used in an emergency rescue is clearly marked. Inside the small door is a lanyard that is pulled to jettison the canopies and rescue the pilot and WSO. The forward left formation light panel is visible as well. On this aircraft, the fixed intake ramp is painted with a checkerboard design, and the forward moveable ramp is just aft (to the right) of this fixed ramp.

A mechanically released ram air turbine (RAT) was located on the left side of the fuselage. The air flow moving past the aircraft turned a generator which supplied electrical power in the event of an emergency. This was a standard feature on all Phantom variants.

Antennas on the spine of the aircraft differed depending on the variant of the Phantom in question and even from aircraft to aircraft. Almost all had the upper TACAN antenna which is the smaller blade antenna on the centerline of the spine just above the Japanese flag. The larger blade antenna, located off to the right of the centerline is the upper UHF antenna. On some aircraft this antenna was also located on the centerline of the spine. Forward is to the right in this photograph.

The large circular antenna on the fairing behind the aft canopy is for the IFF system. Just aft of it is the light which is used to illuminate the refueling receptacle during night in-flight refuelings.

One of the changes made to the Phantom by the Air Force was the removal of the Navy style refueling probe on the forward right side of the fuselage. Instead, an in-flight refueling receptacle, designed for use with the high speed boom system, was located on the spine of the aircraft. The door for this receptacle is shown in the closed position just forward of the aircraft's serial number. This arrangement was common to all Air Force Phantoms.

Ground electrical and hydraulic connections are located under the forward fuselage section.

On either side of the centerline hardpoint are auxiliary intake doors to provide additional cooling air to the engine at slow speeds and during ground operations. The insides of the doors that cover these auxiliary intakes are painted red.

A Phantom takes on fuel through its in-flight refueling receptacle. Also note the bleed air vents on the tops of the inlets. Similar vents are also located on the bottom of the inlets. This photograph also shows the walkway markings on the tops of the inlets and on the wings to good effect. However these varied from aircraft to aircraft. *(Official USAF photo)*

WING DETAILS

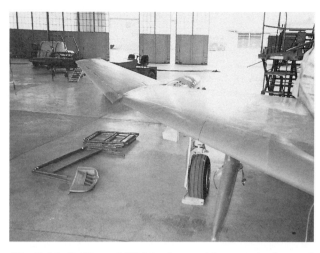

The F-4C, F-4D, and RF-4C, along with several other variants of the Phantom, had three sections of leading edge flaps on each wing. Two were on the inner fixed wing section, and the third was on the outer folding wing panel. At left is a photograph that shows the leading edge of the right wing with the flaps in the retracted or neutral position. At right, the leading edge flaps are in the lowered position.

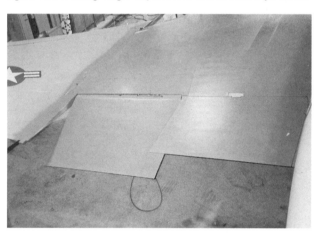
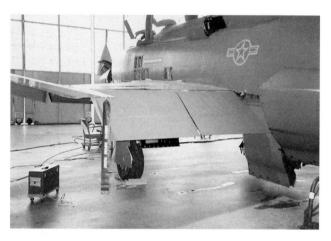

On the trailing edge of each fixed inner wing section were two movable control surfaces. The inboard control surface was a flap, while the outer surface was the aileron. The aileron only moved downward, and it worked in conjunction with the spoiler on the top of the opposite wing which moved upward. (See the middle right photograph on the next page.) In the top view at left, the flap is in the neutral position while the aileron is lowered. At right is a photograph of the flap and aileron on the left wing that is taken from a different angle. In this case both control surfaces are lowered. Under normal situations when a Phantom was on the ground and all systems were shut down, the flap was in the neutral position and the aileron was slightly lowered.

Since the Phantom was originally intended to be a carrier-based aircraft, folding wings were incorporated into its design. The Air Force maintained this feature on all of its variants of the aircraft. Details of the right and left wing fold mechanism and hinges are illustrated in these two photographs.

On the leading edge of each wing tip was a standard position light. The one on the left wing was red and the light on the right wing tip was blue-green. Further back on each wing tip was a formation light panel.

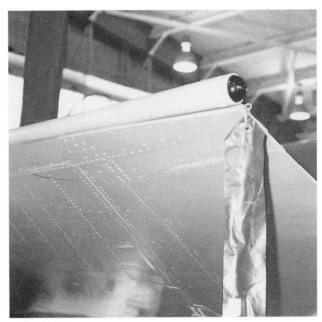

There was also a standard position light on the trailing edge of each wing tip.

Just outboard of the aileron on each inner wing section was the fuel vent for the fuel tanks in the wings.

The spoiler on the top of the right wing is shown here in the raised position. The access panel just forward of the spoiler has been removed for maintenance.

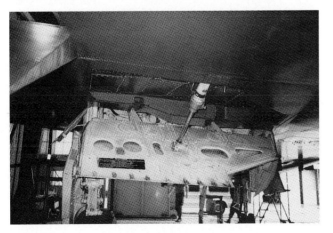

Speed brakes were located just aft of the main landing gear wells under each wing. At left is a close-up of the speed brake under the left wing. The inside of each brake was painted red. At right is a photograph looking up into the speed brake well. Several panels have been removed for maintenance, and the brake has been disconnected from its activating hydraulic piston and cylinder. The interior of the well was usually painted the same color as the underside of the wing.

The right inboard pylon is attached to the wing at this point. The forward locating hole can be seen in the foreground, and the aft end of the pylon is attached to the small post that is visible in the background just forward of the landing gear well. The attach point for the left inboard pylon is the same as this.

The most common external store carried on the outboard wing hardpoints of Phantoms was the 370-gallon fuel tank with its integral pylon. When other stores were carried, a separate pylon was attached to the wing.

The inboard pylons used on the RF-4C were like those used on the Navy Phantoms. These pylons were characterized by their straight leading edge.

The hardpoint for the right outboard pylon is shown here, and the one under the left wing is the same as this one.

This close-up shows the details of the fuel tank and its integral pylon attached to the wing. Note that there is a noticeable gap between the pylon and the wing. The anti-sway brace on the right side of the pylon is also visible.

All other Air Force Phantoms, including the F-4C and F-4D, had a different inboard pylon with a curved leading edge. The device at the trailing edge of the pylon is a chaff/flare dispenser that was added late in the Phantom's operational service. This pylon has a triple ejector rack with three Mk 82, 500-pound bombs.

TAIL DETAILS

Above: Although not originally fitted, the antenna fairing for the AN/APR-25/-26 radar homing and warning system was added to the vertical tail of the F-4C. It can be seen just above the rudder at the aft end of the fin cap. There are two probes on the leading edge of the vertical tail. The top one is a pitot probe, and the lower one is the stabilator feel system pressure head. Just below it on the leading edge is the upper red beacon light. An aft formation light panel is mounted at an angle on each side of the vertical tail.

Above right: The vertical tail on the F-4D was the same as on the F-4C, except that the antenna fairing for the AN/APS-107A RHAW system is shorter and more rounded at the aft end.

Right: There was no RHAW antenna fairing at the top of the vertical tail on the RF-4C. Also note the lack of the pitot probe on the leading edge. This is because the pitot probe on the RF-4C is mounted on the radome. The small white formation light is visible at the aft end of the fin cap at the very top. It is also on other versions of the Phantom, but it is more difficult to see because of the RHAW antenna fairings.

All Phantom variants had intake scoops at the base of the leading edge of the vertical tail. Air taken into the aircraft through these scoops was used to cool the aft electronics bay.

This close-up reveals details of the upper red beacon and the stabilator feel system pressure head on the leading edge of the vertical stabilizer. Note that the pressure head and its mount are left unpainted.

The fuel vent for the fuselage tanks can be seen in this view of the tail that was taken from below and behind the aircraft. The two "eyes" on the tail cone are nodes for the RHAW system.

The tail cone covers the parabrake compartment and opens as shown here. The parabrake has been removed to reveal the actuator that forces the chute out of the compartment during landing rollout.

The horizontal stabilators on the F-4C, F-4D, and RF-4C were identical, and did not have the leading edge slot that characterized later aircraft. Unlike the Navy's F-4B/-N, the slots were not retrofitted to these three variants.

This underside view of the left stabilator shows the arrowhead-shaped reinforcement strip common to Air Force (but not Navy or Marine) Phantoms. The one on the upper surface of the same stabilator can be seen in the photograph at left.

Although not intended for carrier use, Air Force Phantoms retained the same arresting hook to be used for emergency barrier landings on runways. At left is an overall view of the hook from the left, and at right is a close-up of where the end of the hook attaches to the underside of the tail section. Vents for the aft fuselage section are also visible.

COLOR GALLERY
EJECTION SEAT DETAILS & COLORS

  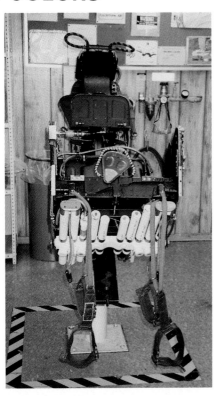

The Martin-Baker Mk H7 ejection seat was standard in Air Force Phantoms, although the similar Mk H5 was original equipment in the F-4C and RF-4C until retrofitted. The front and back views are of a packed seat that is ready for installation in the aircraft. At right is an unpacked seat that is tilted up to reveal the rocket motors that propel the seat out of the aircraft. Leg restraint garters are also visible in this view. The seat could be fired by using a handle on the front of the seat or by pulling the overhead rings. The personal parachute was located in the headrest, and the survival kit was in the seat cushion.

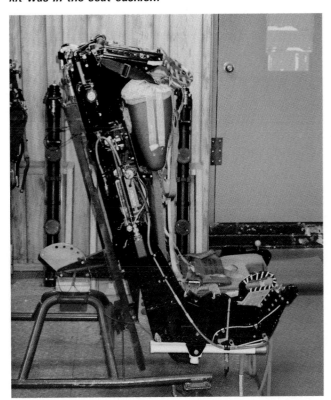 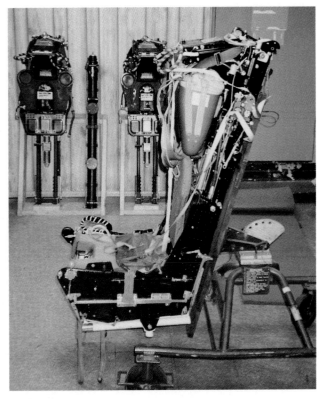

Right and left side views show more details and colors of the Mk H7 seat.

F-4C & F-4D PAINT SCHEMES

Beginning on this page, and continuing on the next, is a review of the various official paint schemes used on the F-4C and F-4D variants of the Phantom. The two photographs above show the colors and markings of one of the first two Navy F-4Bs used by the Air Force to evaluate the Phantom. The Navy's light gull gray over white paint scheme is clearly illustrated from above and below. The subsequent twenty-seven F-4Bs used by the Air Force, as well as early production F-4Cs and RF-4Cs, were delivered in this paint scheme. (Both National Archives)

The Air Force's standard camouflage scheme can be seen on this F-4D which is enroute to its target in Vietnam. The camouflage pattern on the upper and vertical surfaces of the aircraft were painted in dark green (FS 34079), medium green (FS 34102), and tan (FS 30219). Undersurfaces were painted a very light gray (FS 36622). The standard camouflage scheme was first used on USAF Phantoms and many other aircraft early in the Vietnam war, and remained the norm for several years thereafter. (National Archives)

Shortly after the war in Vietnam, the wraparound scheme was adopted. For this camouflage scheme, the two greens and the tan that were used for the standard camouflage scheme were also painted in a pattern on the lower surfaces of the aircraft, and the light gray was deleted. The wraparound camouflage scheme is illustrated on this F-4D from the 906th TFG.

A line-up of Phantoms at an air show reveals several different paint schemes. Closest to the camera is an aircraft from the Oregon Air National Guard in the overall ADC gray scheme. Phantoms assigned to units with a primary air defense mission were usually painted in this gray (FS 16473).
(Flightleader)

The European 1 camouflage scheme used a similar pattern as the wrap-around scheme, however there were some differences. Dark green (FS 34079) and medium green (FS 34102) were still specified, but were in different locations within the pattern. Gray (FS 36081) replaced the tan, but again was used at different places within the pattern. This F-4D was the wing commander's aircraft from the 482nd TFW of the Air Force Reserve.
(Flightleader)

The last official paint scheme seen on F-4Cs and F-4Ds was a two or three-tone gray scheme often using the same grays that were specified for use on the F-16. Although the darker gray was almost always Gunship Gray (FS 36118), the lighter grays sometimes varied. At times, only one lighter shade of gray was used, but in other cases, two lighter shades were applied to the aircraft. The patterns for the grays also varied to an extent from unit to unit and even from aircraft to aircraft. For example, on some aircraft the anti-glare panel was painted in the darker gray and extended to a black radome. On other aircraft, the darker gray wrapped around the upper portion of the radome which was otherwise painted a lighter gray, and on still other aircraft there was no anti-glare panel. An F-4C from the Oregon Air National Guard is shown here in one of these paint schemes. In this case, three different shades are used, with the lightest color having been applied to the radome, pylons, and the undersides of the forward fuselage. Note how this lighter gray extends back past the radome onto the forward fuselage section. Compare this scheme to the two-tone gray F-4D which is illustrated on the front cover.
(Grove via Flightleader)

F-4D COCKPIT DETAILS & COLORS

The layout of the cockpit of a given aircraft can change over the years as new equipment is added or updated. At times, the changes may be made to all aircraft of a given type, while in other cases the modifications may begin with a certain production block. There are also instances when the changes are made only to selected aircraft. Official drawings usually show "standard" configurations with items identified in keys. Examples of these drawings are included on pages 12 and 13 for the F-4C and pages 16 and 17 for the F-4D. However, the photographs on this page illustrate one major change made to seventy-two F-4Ds which received the AN/ARN-92 LORAN system. Externally, these aircraft could be distinguished by the "towel rack" antenna on their spine, but there were changes made inside the cockpits as well. The photograph at left shows the front cockpit in a "standard" F-4D, while the rear cockpit is illustrated at right.

(Left Roth, right Henning via Roth)

The cockpits in an F-4D equipped with the LORAN system are shown here. Again, the front cockpit is in the photograph at left, and the rear cockpit is shown in the right photograph. Changes in the front cockpit appear to be relatively minor, while those in the rear cockpit are much more extensive.

(Both Roth)

F-4C & F-4D RADAR DETAILS & COLORS

The F-4C was fitted with the AN/APG-100 radar, which could be pulled out of the nose of the aircraft on rails when maintenance was required. These two photographs provide a good look at the colors and details of the antenna and its associated equipment as crewmen service the system. **(Both are official Air Force photos)**

The interior of the radome as installed on an F-4C is shown at left. The one on the F-4D was essentially identical. At right is a photograph looking aft into the forward section of the nose with the radar removed. The rails on which the radar was mounted are clearly visible at the top of the opening. These rails telescoped out from the nose section to provide easy access to the radar as seen in the photographs above and below.

The F-4D was fitted with the AN/APG-109A radar which was very similar in appearance to the AN/APG-100 used in the F-4C. One noticeable difference is the number of dipoles on the antenna dish.

(Left author, right official Air Force photo)

RF-4C PAINT SCHEMES

Paint schemes used on the RF-4C paralleled those used on other Air Force variants of the Phantom. The first few RF-4Cs were delivered in the Navy light gull gray over white scheme as shown here.

(Official Air Force photo)

Next, RF-4Cs were painted in the standard Air Force camouflage scheme shown on this aircraft is from the 67th TRW. The wraparound version of this scheme was also used on RF-4Cs.

(Official Air Force photo)

This RF-4C from the Kentucky Air National Guard is painted in the European 1 camouflage scheme.

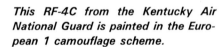

The last RF-4Cs in service were painted in the two-tone gray scheme, and it was in this scheme that the recon Phantoms served during Operations Desert Shield and Desert Storm. This particular RF-4C is from the 117th TRW of the Alabama Air National Guard, and it was painted in special markings to commemorate the thirty-fifth anniversary of the Phantom's first flight. These markings were designed by Don Spering who also headed up the crew that painted the aircraft.

(Don Spering/AIR)

RF-4C COCKPIT DETAILS & COLORS

FRONT COCKPIT

REAR COCKPIT

The photographs on this page were all taken in the front and rear cockpits of an RF-4C shortly after it returned from Operation Desert Storm. They illustrate the cockpit details as they were during the final three years of the RF-4C's operational service. At left is the instrument panel in the forward cockpit. A view from the opposite side of the aircraft appears on the rear cover. At right is the main instrument panel in the rear cockpit. Note that a control column, throttles, and basic flight instruments are in the rear cockpit. There are also rudder pedals in the rear cockpit, but they are not visible in this photograph.

The left console in the forward cockpit is shown at left, while the left console in the rear cockpit is illustrated at right.

At left is a photograph of the right console in the pilot's cockpit, while at right is the right console in the rear cockpit.

AN/APQ-172 RADAR DETAILS & COLORS

The AN/APQ-99 radar was originally installed under the smaller radome in the RF-4C. It was subsequently replaced with the AN/APQ-172, which was almost identical in appearance and which is illustrated on this page. Some of the antenna dishes were gold, while others were gray as shown in these two photos. The radome was hinged at the top and opened upward rather than to the side as on the F-4C and F-4D. The oval shape of the radar dish is illustrated at left, while the photograph at right reveals right side details of the radar set.

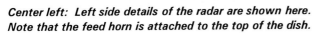

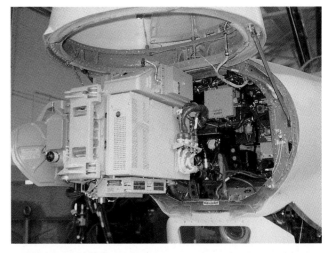

Center left: Left side details of the radar are shown here. Note that the feed horn is attached to the top of the dish.

Center right: Rather than rolling out of the aircraft on rails as on the F-4C and F-4D, the APQ-99 radar was hinged on its right side and could be opened out of the aircraft.

Right: This unusual view looks straight up into the raised radome on an RF-4C and reveals the colors and the details of its interior.

F-4C, F-4D, RF-4C DIMENSIONS

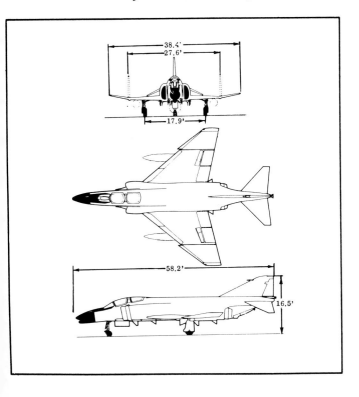

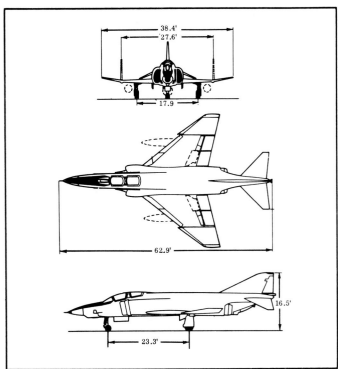

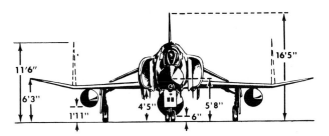

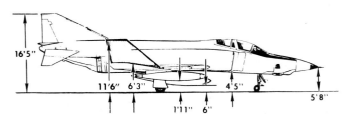

Courtesy of the U.S.A.F.

DIMENSION DATA

DIMENSION	ACTUAL	1/72nd SCALE	1/48th SCALE	1/32nd SCALE
LENGTH (F-4C/D)	58.2'	9.70"	14.55"	21.83"
LENGTH (RF-4C)	62.9'	10.48"	15.73"	23.59"
WINGSPAN	38.4'	6.40"	9.60"	14.40"
WINGS FOLDED	27.6'	4.60"	6.90"	10.35"
HEIGHT	16.5'	2.75"	4.13"	6.19"
WHEEL TREAD	17.9'	2.98"	4.48"	6.71"
WHEEL TRACK	23.3'	3.88"	5.83"	8.74"

WING DATA:

Incidence . . . . 1°
Dihedral (Inner Panel) . . . . 0°
Dihedral (Outer Panel) . . . . 12°
Sweepback (25% chord) . . . . 45°
Area . . . . 530 sq. ft.
Aspect Ratio 2.82
M.A.C. . . . . 16.04 ft.
Wing Section (Parallel to Center Line)
Root . . . . NACA 0006.4-64 (Mod)
Fold . . . . NACA 0004-64 (Mod)
Tip . . . . NACA 0003-64 (Mod)

F-4C & F-4D 1/72nd SCALE FIVE VIEW DRAWINGS

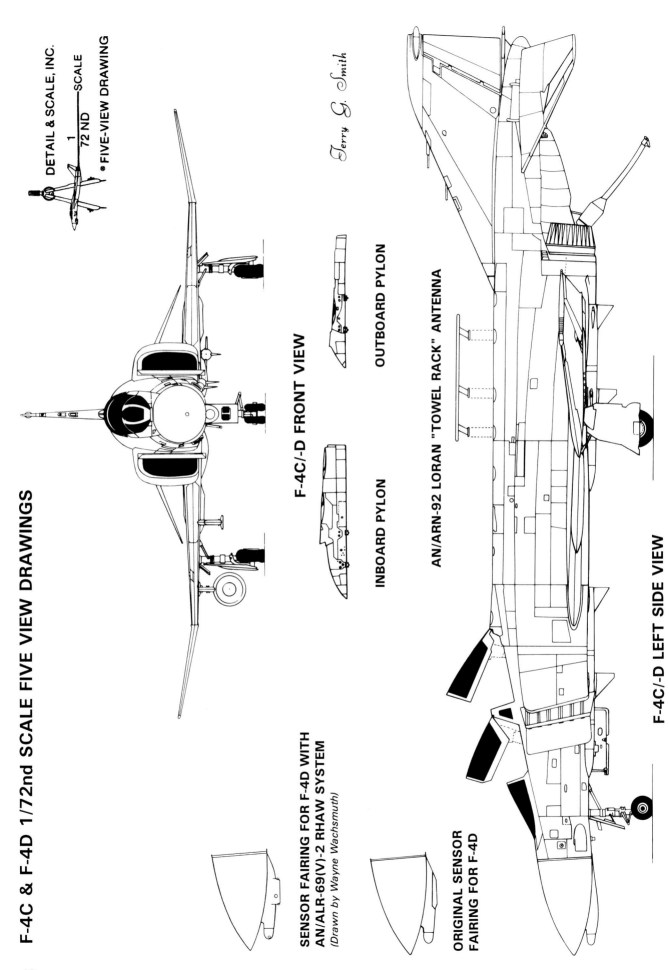

DETAIL & SCALE, INC.

1
——— SCALE
72 ND

● FIVE-VIEW DRAWING

Jerry G. Smith

F-4C/-D FRONT VIEW

INBOARD PYLON

OUTBOARD PYLON

AN/ARN-92 LORAN "TOWEL RACK" ANTENNA

F-4C/-D LEFT SIDE VIEW

SENSOR FAIRING FOR F-4D WITH AN/ALR-69(V)-2 RHAW SYSTEM
(Drawn by Wayne Wachsmuth)

ORIGINAL SENSOR FAIRING FOR F-4D

42

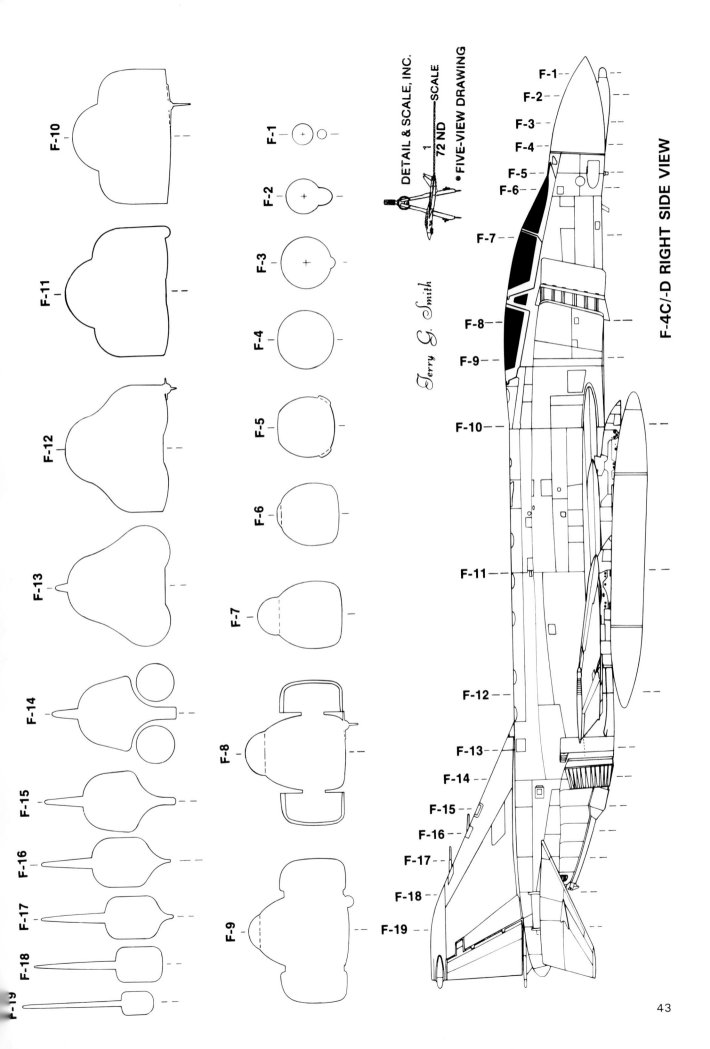

DETAIL & SCALE, INC.

1 / 72ND SCALE

* FIVE-VIEW DRAWING

Jerry G. Smith

F-4C/-D RIGHT SIDE VIEW

F-1
F-2
F-3
F-4
F-5
F-6
F-7
F-8
F-9
F-10
F-11
F-12
F-13
F-14
F-15
F-16
F-17
F-18
F-19

F-4C/-D TOP VIEW

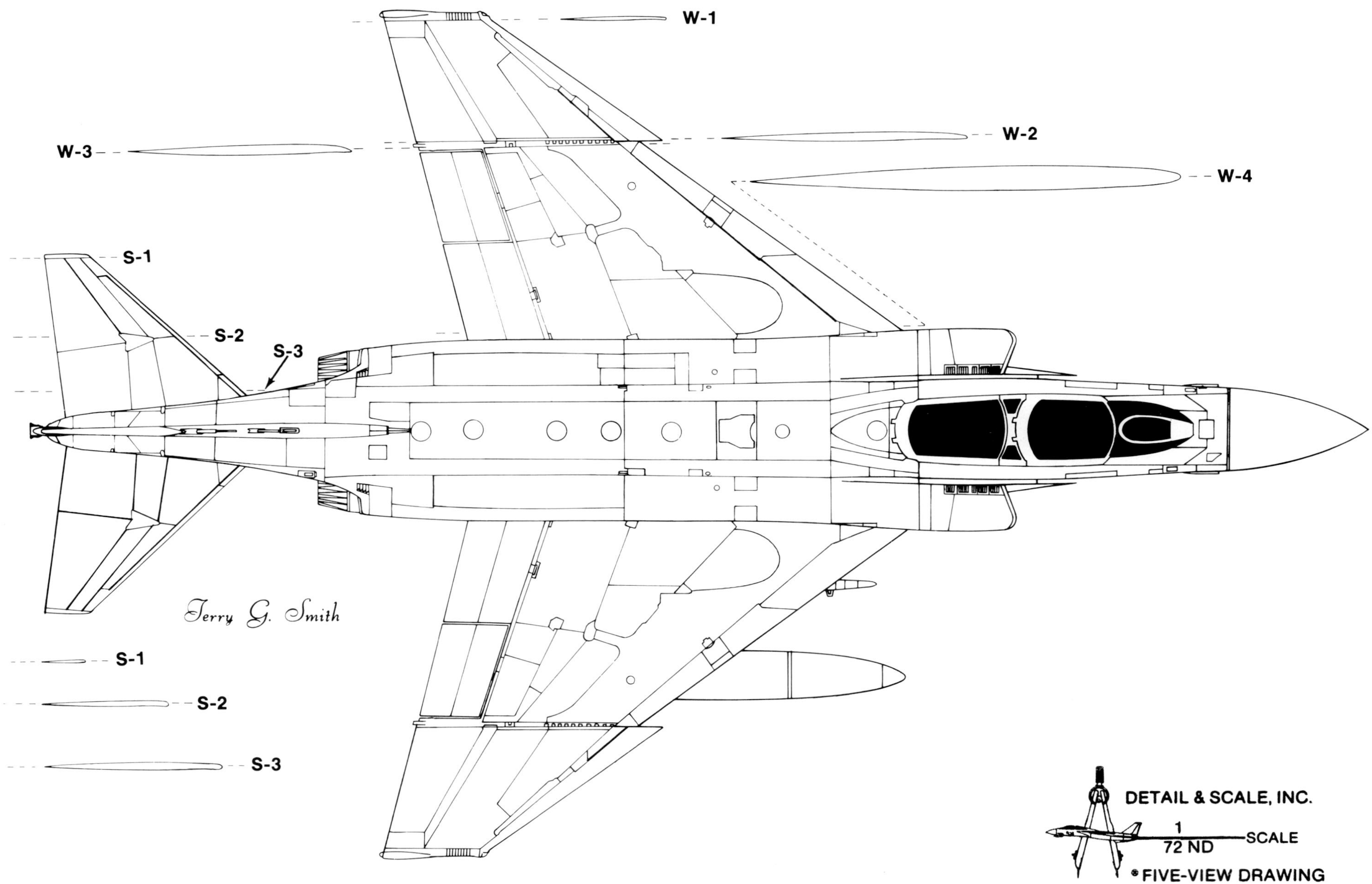

W-4

W-2

W-1

W-3

S-1

S-2

S-3

Jerry G. Smith

S-1

S-2

S-3

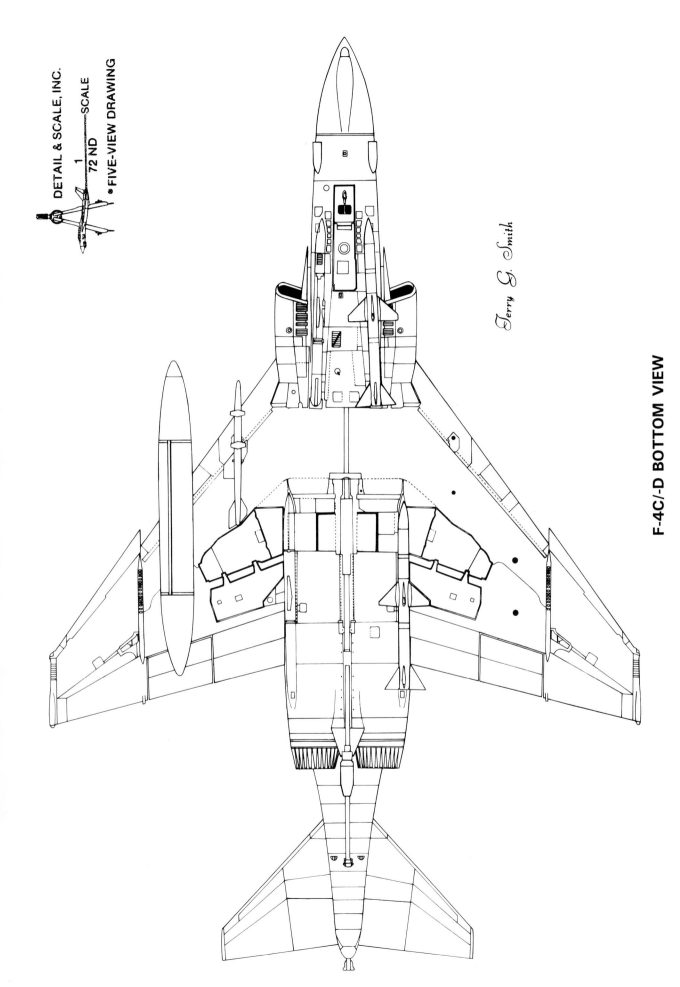

Jerry G. Smith

F-4C/-D BOTTOM VIEW

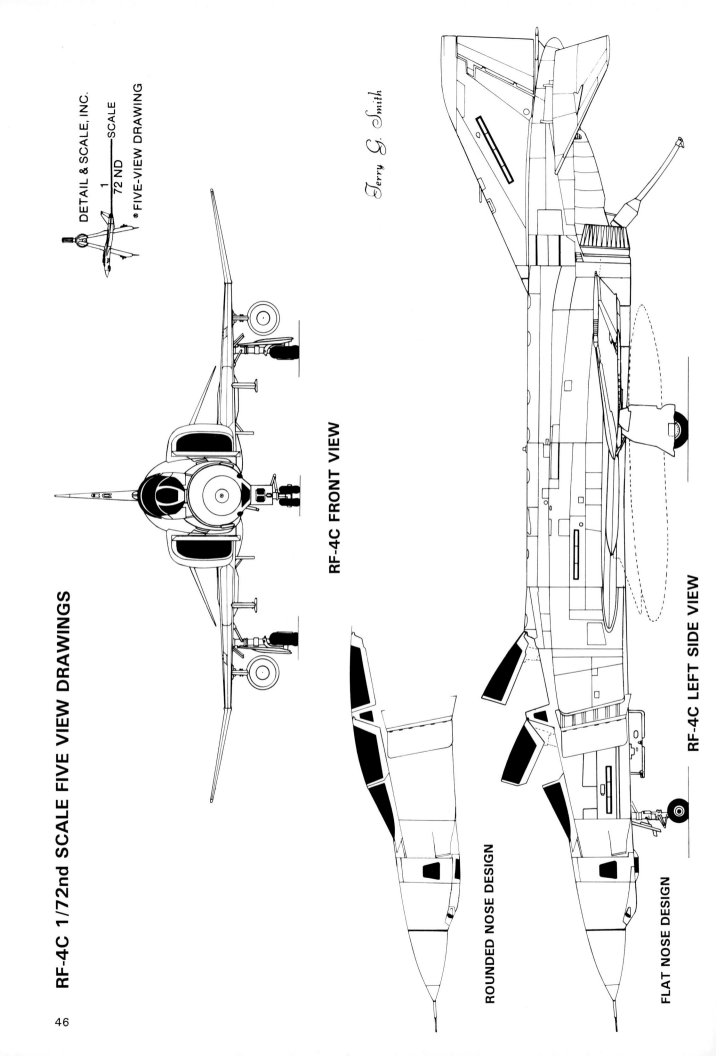

RF-4C 1/72nd SCALE FIVE VIEW DRAWINGS

DETAIL & SCALE, INC.

1
72 ND — SCALE

® FIVE-VIEW DRAWING

Jerry G. Smith

RF-4C FRONT VIEW

RF-4C LEFT SIDE VIEW

ROUNDED NOSE DESIGN

FLAT NOSE DESIGN

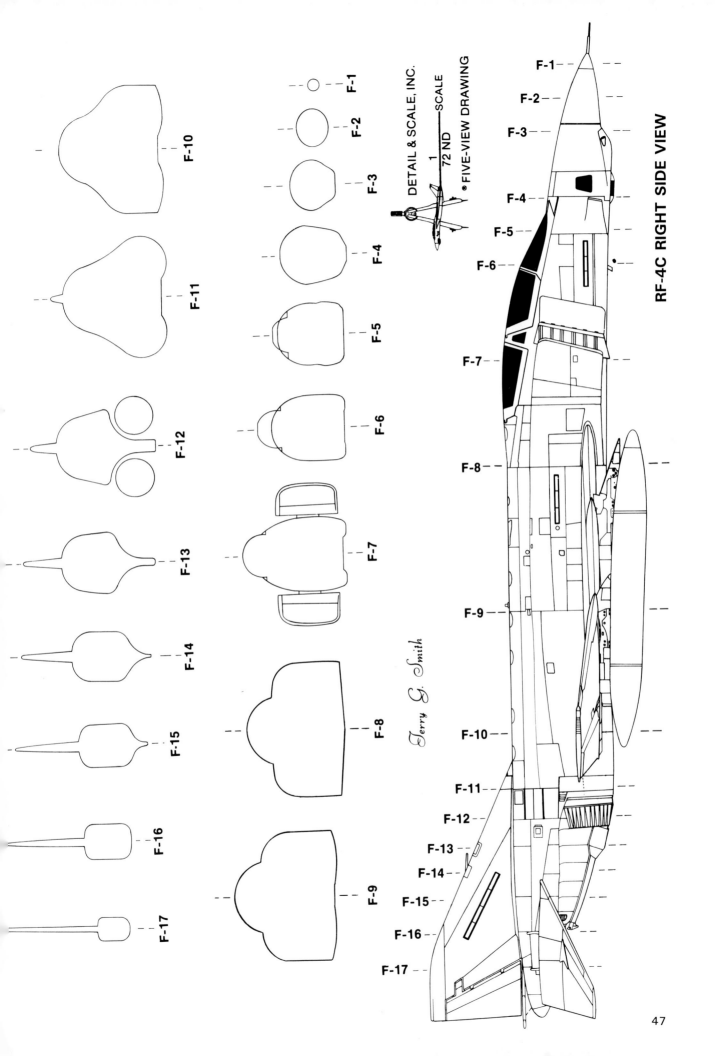

F-10 F-11 F-12 F-13 F-14 F-15 F-16 F-17

F-1 F-2 F-3 F-4 F-5 F-6 F-7 F-8 F-9

DETAIL & SCALE, INC.

1
72 ND SCALE

*FIVE-VIEW DRAWING

Jerry G. Smith

RF-4C RIGHT SIDE VIEW

F-1 F-2 F-3 F-4 F-5 F-6 F-7 F-8 F-9 F-10 F-11 F-12 F-13 F-14 F-15 F-16 F-17

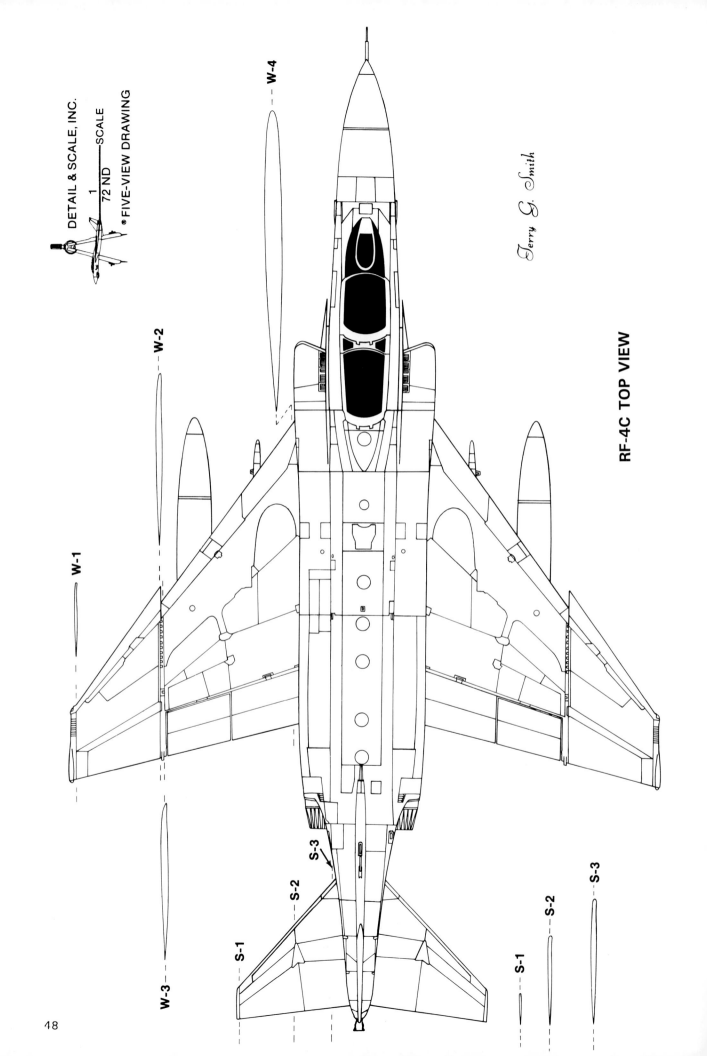

Jerry G. Smith

W-4

W-2

W-1

W-3

S-3

S-2

S-1

S-1

S-2

S-3

RF-4C TOP VIEW

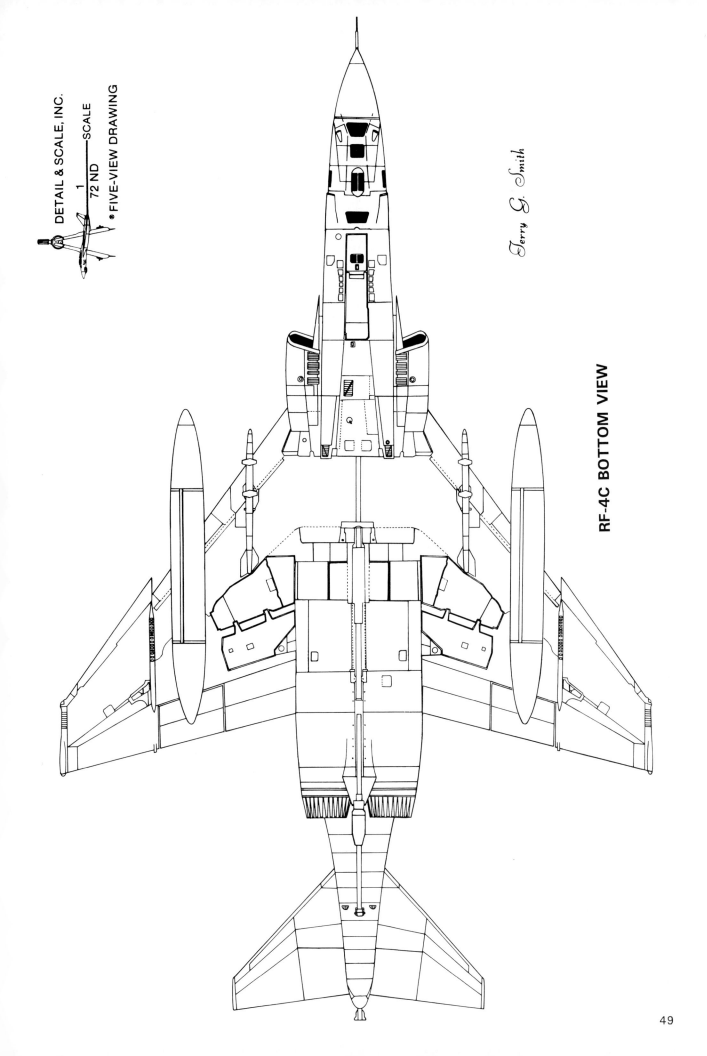

DETAIL & SCALE, INC.

1
72 ND — SCALE

® FIVE-VIEW DRAWING

Jerry G. Smith

RF-4C BOTTOM VIEW

F-4C & F-4D ARMAMENT

During their operational life, the fighter variants of the Phantom carried almost every type of air-delivered ordnance in the U. S. arsenal. From tiny practice bombs to nuclear weapons, and from rocket pods to anti-radiation missiles, there were very few munitions that the Phantom was not certified to carry. To dramatize the F-4's ordnance carrying capability, the Air Force released this publicity photograph of an early F-4C with a variety of weapons positioned with it. Yet this picture illustrates only a fraction of the types of stores the Phantom would actually carry operationally. Many additional weapons would also be tested on the Phantom over the years, although they would not be carried operationally. Space limitations prohibit an in-depth study of all of the types of ordnance carried on the F-4C and F-4D in this publication, and such a presentation is beyond the scope of this book. However, some of the ordnance carried on F-4Cs and F-4Ds is illustrated on this and the following three pages. *(Official Air Force photo)*

GUN PODS

Having no internal cannon, the F-4C and F-4D had to carry externally mounted gun pods. Two similar 20-mm pods were used. The first of these was the SUU-16 shown here. It was powered by a ram air turbine (RAT) that opened into the airstream when the gun was ready to fire. An armorer is seen working on the RAT in this photograph. *(Official Air Force photo)*

The SUU-23, often misidentified as the SUU-16, had an internal electrical motor driven by gun gas and therefore did not require a RAT to provide the electrical power. Like the SUU-16, the SUU-23 was based on the six-barrel Vulcan cannon system. Note the air intake above the forward natural metal portion of the gun which is a distinctive identifying feature of the SUU-23. This gun pod also had two different caps for its aft end. One was streamlined, and the other was "stubby" as shown in this photograph. This cap allowed the pod to be carried on the inboard wing pylon of the Phantom with clearance for the landing gear door. Both gun pods could carry 1,200 rounds of ammunition and had thirty-inch lug spacing. *(Official Air Force photo)*

AIR-TO-AIR MISSILES

The design of fighter variants of the Phantom included four recessed bays under the fuselage for the radar guided AIM-7 Sparrow missile. These missiles were intended to be the aircraft's main air-to-air weapon. However, a mix of radar guided and infrared guided missiles was desirable, and the Air Force certified the use of the AIM-4D Falcon missiles on the aircraft. Four Falcons are seen on the inboard pylons of this F-4C. The launch rail is L shaped, with one Falcon directly below the pylon and another positioned to the inside of each pylon. Problems with the AIM-4D led to its replacement with the AIM-9 Sidewinder.
(Official Air Force photo)

The AIR-2 Genie unguided rocket, which carried a nuclear warhead, was also evaluated for use on the Phantom, however it was not used in operational service with the aircraft. The same aircraft shown above is seen here again with two Genies attached to its inboard wing pylons. AIM-7 Sparrows are in their bays under the fuselage.   (Official Air Force photo)

Many different variants of the Sidewinder air-to-air guided missiles have been carried by the F-4C and F-4D versions of the Phantom. The earliest of these was the AIM-9B seen here. This missile was basically a tail chase weapon and was used with some success in Vietnam. Sidewinders were carried on launch rails which were shoulder mounted on the inboard wing pylons as illustrated here. An ALQ-71 ECM pod can be seen beneath the pylon.

Improved versions of the Sidewinders were carried by Phantoms over the years. Shown here is a practice AIM-9P on an F-4D in 1984. Late in their operational life, some F-4Ds carried the AIM-9L and AIM-9M, and at least nine RF-4Cs were also wired to fire these latest versions of the Sidewinder.

The AIM-7E was used in Vietnam, and was found to be less than reliable. The black stripe on the missile's wing indicates that this is an AIM-7E-2 version.

Ground crew personnel load a training version of the Sparrow missile into the left aft missile bay on an F-4D.

STANDARD BOMBS

Fuze wires are installed on Mk 82, 500-pound bombs in preparation for loading on an F-4C. These bombs have the standard low drag tail sections fitted. (Official Air Force photo)

Right: High drag Mk 82s were also carried by Phantoms. These included the earlier Snakeye versions and the later Air Inflatable Retard (AIR) bombs shown here on an F-4D. Also note the chaff/flare dispenser on the side of the pylon at its aft end. These dispensers were not originally equipment on Phantoms, but they were added to each side of both inboard pylons late in the aircraft's service life.

Above left: Moving up one size from the Mk 82 was the M117, 750-pound bomb. Three are shown here on a triple ejector rack attached to the inboard left pylon. The AIM-9Bs, which are shoulder mounted on the pylon, could not have been fired until after the bombs had been dropped.

Above right: The next larger bomb carried by Phantoms was the Mk 83, 1000-pound bomb shown here. Although used by the Air Force in Vietnam, this weapon is now used only by the Navy and Marines.

(Official Air Force photo)

Right: BDU-33 practice bombs had ballistic characteristics which were similar to the real thing, and they were usually painted solid blue. Orange Mk 106 practice bombs simulated retarded nuclear weapons.

SMART BOMBS

The Phantom was the first operational fighter to deliver laser guided bombs (LGB) in combat. Here an aircraft of the 8th TFW prepares to taxi out for a mission over North Vietnam. It has an unusual asymmetrical ordnance load. On the right outboard hardpoint is a 370-gallon fuel tank, and on the right inboard pylon is a GBU-10A/B LGB. The centerline station carries a 600-gallon fuel tank, and two AIM-7E-2 Sparrows are in the aft bays for self defense. The large AVQ-10 Pave Knife designator pod is on the left inboard pylon, while a second GBU-10A/B is on the left outboard station. The GBU-10 series of LGBs used Mk 84, 2000-pound bombs for warheads. (Official Air Force photo)

Right: Smaller GBU-12 LGBs are on the left inboard wing pylon of this Phantom. The GBU-12 series of LGBs were based on the Mk 82, 500-pound bomb. Note the AVQ-23 Pave Spike designator pod in the left forward Sparrow missile bay. Because this smaller pod could be carried in a missile bay instead of on one of the pylons, more fuel or ordnance could be loaded on the aircraft.
(Official Air Force photo)

Electro-optically guided bombs could also be delivered by Phantoms. In this photograph, an F-4D is shown with two GBU-8 homing bomb systems (HOBOS). This weapon used the Mk 84, 2000-pound bomb as its warhead. The GBU-8 was evaluated but not used in combat. The GBU-9 (which used the M118 bomb as its warhead) was used operationally in Vietnam.
(Official Air Force photo)

Left: The GBU-15(V)-1 was also tested on some F-4Ds as shown here. However, the only Phantom unit to have them operationally was one wing of F-4Es. The GBU-15 was used very successfully by the F-111F during the Gulf War.

RF-4C

This early production RF-4C is painted in the Navy's light gull gray over white scheme and carries a candy striped instrumentation probe during flight testing. Two early style wing tanks and a centerline tank are fitted.

(National Archives)

Between 1954 and 1957, the Air Force acquired 388 RF-84F Thunderflash tactical reconnaissance aircraft, but the rapidly advancing technology of that time period rendered them obsolete before the final RF-84F rolled off of the production line. As a result, these aircraft were quickly turned over to Reserve and Guard units. Beginning in 1957, 201 RF-101A/-C Voodoos were produced, but tactical reconnaissance assets within the Air Force were still in short supply. Proposed reconnaissance variants of other fighters, including the F-100 and F-105, had not advanced past the experimental stage.

Having been impressed with the Phantom's performance characteristics in 1961 and early 1962, the Air Force realized that the F-4's large airframe could be converted into an aircraft that would be an excellent reconnaissance platform. The wisdom of this decision is evidenced by the fact that the resulting RF-4C served the U. S. military longer than any other Phantom variant.

On 29 May, 1962, Specific Operational Requirement (SOR) 196 was issued, and it spelled out just what the Air Force wanted their reconnaissance variant of the Phantom to be. Although the letter contract for the F-4C had been issued two months earlier, the SOR for the RF-4C actually predated the SOR for the F-4C by almost three months. Among other things, SOR 196 included the requirement that the RF-4C be capable of delivering nuclear weapons.

Since no F-4Cs had yet been produced, six Navy F-4Bs were pulled off the line and converted to test and evaluation RF-4Cs. These aircraft had the elongated and slimmer nose sections that would become standard with the RF-4C, and they had varying amounts of equipment installed. The first two of these were prototypes, while the remaining four were completed more to production standards. Like the prototypes, these four were intended to serve only as test and evaluation aircraft. A mock-up inspection was held on 29 October, 1962, just as the Cuban Missile Crisis was dramatizing the importance of tactical reconnaissance aircraft. Events leading to the initial operational capability of the RF-4C and its combat debut then proceeded very quickly.

The maiden flight of the first prototype aircraft was made ahead of schedule on 8 August, 1963. The second prototype, and the first to have any camera equipment, followed on 30 September. The third aircraft was the first to be fitted with a forward looking radar and other avionics equipment, and it was flying by 18 November. The first production RF-4C made its initial flight on 18 May, 1964, and the aircraft entered operational service the following September. In August 1965, the 16th Tactical Reconnaissance Squadron became the first unit to be declared operationally ready. Less than two months later, and with war in Vietnam quickly escalating, RF-4Cs were rushed to SEA on 31 October, 1965. By the end of the year, twenty of the new aircraft were "in country" and flying missions. More than a quarter of a century later, RF-4Cs would again go to war in the skies over the Middle East.

Inside the elongated nose of the RF-4C were three camera stations where a variety of cameras could be arranged to cover forward, vertical, and oblique angles from the aircraft. For night photography, photo flash cartridges could be ejected from compartments in the tail section of the aircraft. In-flight film processing was originally designed into the system, and a film cassette could be jettisoned and parachuted to personnel on the ground. However, this system proved to be less than satisfactory, and it was subsequently removed from the aircraft. The AN/AAS-18 infrared sensor equipment also had to be improved and was later replaced with the AN/AAS-18A. The AN/AVD-2 laser reconnaissance set could also be carried in camera station two, but its use has now been discontinued.

The Texas Instruments AN/APQ-99 radar was fitted under the radome to provide ground mapping as well as terrain and collision avoidance. It was later replaced with the AN/APQ-172 which was almost identical in physical appearance. (Photographs of the AN/APQ-172 can be found on page 40.) These forward looking radars provided a 100-degree scan width ahead of the aircraft, while the AN/APQ-102 side-looking radar covered twenty degrees on each side.

The General Dynamics HIAC-1 camera, which had a focal length of sixty-six inches, was fitted into the large G-139 pod. With only minimal ground clearance, this pod could be carried on the centerline station of an RF-4C. Although this camera offered outstanding long range photography, it was not used extensively with the RF-4C. During Operations Desert Shield and Desert Storm, anoth-

The huge General Dynamics G-139 pod could be carried on the centerline station of the RF-4C, and it was fitted with a HIAC-1, 66-inch focal length camera. Late in the operational life of the RF-4C, the KS-127 camera, also with a 66-inch focal length, would be carried inside the nose of the aircraft, thus eliminating the need for this large external pod. **(National Archives)**

A few RF-4Cs were fitted with the Litton TEREC antenna in place of cameras in station two. This antenna was designed to locate and identify radars associated with enemy air defense gun and missile systems. The antenna can be seen here on RF-4C, 69-368, when the aircraft was assigned to the 38th TRS of the 26th TRW. **(Rotramel)**

er camera with sixty-six inches of focal length was carried in the nose section of the RF-4C. This was the KS-127 camera, and it provided excellent photography of Iraqi installations and troop movements in Kuwait. The camera bay had to be modified to accept this large camera, and only selected RF-4Cs were modified to employ it. Two aiming devices were added to the canopy rails inside the rear cockpit, and this was the only external feature that indicated that an RF-4C was modified to carry this camera. As of this writing, one of the cameras remains with the 106th Reconnaissance Squadron of the Alabama ANG, and a second camera has been assigned to the 192nd Reconnaissance Squadron of the Nevada ANG.

Twenty-four AN/ALQ-125 Tactical Electronic Reconnaissance (TEREC) kits were produced, and most of these, were distributed to selected RF-4C squadrons. The remainder were used for test and evaluation purposes and for spares. This system was designed to locate and identify radars associated with air defense gun and missile systems. When installed, the TEREC antenna was visible forward of the nose landing gear.

The AN/ARN-92 LORAN navigation system was added to twenty RF-4Cs during the war in Vietnam. Like the F-4Ds, which were also fitted with this system, these RF-4Cs were characterized by the system's "towel rack" antenna on the spine. Later, all surviving aircraft received the AN/ARN-101 avionics system which could be identified by the elongated diamond shaped antenna on the spine.

Thirty-nine RF-4Cs were modified to employ the AN/APQ-26 Pave Tack system which is more commonly associated with the F-111F. It was intended that these RF-4Cs would act as strike control and reconnaissance (SCAR) aircraft which would designate targets for weapons carried by other types of strike aircraft. The Pave Tack pod was carried on the centerline station of the RF-4C, and it was refered to as "Pave Drag" by the aircrews.

Although several types of conventional ordnance was evaluated on RF-4Cs assigned to test squadrons, the only types of air-to-ground weapons ever certified for the aircraft to carry operationally were B28, B43, and B57 special (nuclear) weapons. For practice purposes, an SUU-21/A dispenser could be used, and all of these stores were carried on the aircraft's centerline station. Late in the aircraft's service life, a few were wired to launch AIM-9M Sidewinder missiles from their inboard wing pylons. As of December 1993, the 106th RS had nine aircraft equipped to fire this missile. This was the first and only air-to-air weapon to arm the RF-4C during its thirty-plus years of service.

A total of 505 RF-4Cs were ordered by the Air Force including the six reconfigured Navy F-4Bs. Of this number, 499 aircraft were accepted by the Air Force. Spain recieved six RF-4Cs and eighteen were transferred to the Republic of Korea. All were ex-USAF aircraft, and no RF-4Cs were produced specifically for a foreign user.

During Operation Desert Storm, launch rails with AIM-9 Sidewinders were fitted to the inboard pylons of a few RF-4Cs. Although they could not be fired at that time, tests had shown the compatibility of the Sidewinder with the RF-4C. At this writing, the 117th TRW has actually wired nine of its aircraft to fire the Sidewinder, thus giving the RF-4C a self defense air-to-air weapon for the first time in its operational career. One of the unit's aircraft is shown here with a training missile on its right inboard pylon. (Ashmore)

RF-4C DETAILS

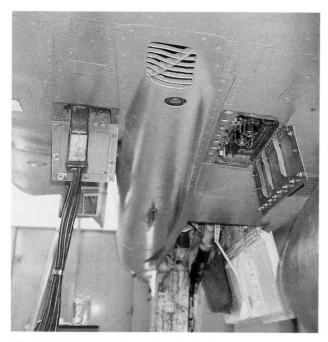 

The RF-4C does not have the missile bays for the AIM-7 Sparrow air-to-air missiles like fighter versions of the Phantom do. In place of the forward bays are the fairings shown here. Each has a vent at the aft end. In the photograph at left, ground-based electrical power can be seen connected to the aircraft. To the right of the fairing are hydraulic connections. Both photographs were taken from under the center of the aircraft looking forward. Rather than having fairings, the underside of the aft fuselage section is flat where the missile bays would be on a fighter variant of the aircraft.

The angle-of-attack probe is on the right side of the nose of the RF-4C instead of the left as seen on the F-4C and F-4D. Also note the different shape of the air conditioning intake as compared to that used on the F-4C and F-4D.

On each side of the rear fuselage of the RF-4C is a compartment for flares that are used for in-flight photography. The inside of the compartment is painted red, while the flare holder is natural metal. At left is a close-up of the compartment on the right side of an RF-4C, while at right, an airman loads flares into a dispenser prior to installation in the aircraft. The open compartment can be seen in the background.   (Left author, right official Air Force photo)

This side-by-side comparison shows the two different nose designs used on the RF-4C. At left is the original configuration with the flat underside, while at right is the nose with the rounded underside. The rounded design did not actually replace the flat design, since both configurations remained in production until deliveries of the RF-4C ended. However, the flat design was used in considerably greater numbers. (Both Rotramel)

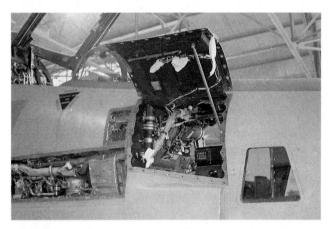

An open access door and two removed panels on the right side of the nose section reveal some of the wiring and plumbing that lies just below the aircraft's skin.

More opened areas on the left side of the nose section are shown here. The two pairs of small dots, located just forward of the inlet ramp and also just above it, are buttons used for raising and lowering the canopies.

Thirty-nine RF-4Cs were modified to carry the AN/AVQ-26 Pave Tack system which is most often associated with the F-111F aircraft. The Pave Tack pod was carried on the RF-4C's centerline station as shown here. In the strike control and reconnaissance (SCAR) role, the RF-4C would used this pod to designate targets for smart weapons carried by other aircraft. (Rotramel)

The RF-4Cs which were modified to employ the long range KS-127 camera could be idendified by the two sighting devices located on the inside of the rear canopy frame. The KS-127, which has a focal length of 66-inches, was used extensively during Operations Desert Shield and Desert Storm.

CAMERA BAY DETAILS

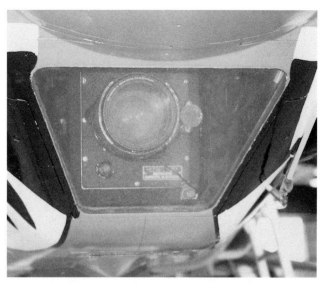

This close-up shows a KS-87 camera installed in the number one or forward looking camera position.

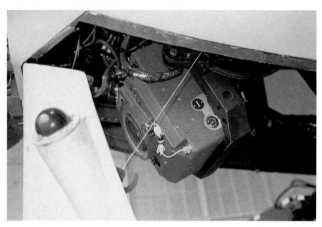

The windows for the various forward-looking and vertical cameras can be seen in this view. The forward-looking camera is mounted in station one just behind the nearest window. It is mounted at an angle just aft of the radome. The middle two windows are for station two, which is the low altitude camera station, while the larger aft window is for the high altitude vertical camera in station three.

With the forward camera bay door open, the KS-87 camera can be seen on its mount.

Several camera configurations can be fitted into station two. In one case, a KA-56 low-altitude panoramic camera can be installed to shoot through the third window back from the front as seen in the top left photograph on this page. But the two side-looking windows shown in these photographs can also be used by cameras in station two. One alternative is to use two KS-87 cameras with one positioned in each window. A more common option is to mount a single camera which can be rotated to shoot out either of the side windows as required. The large KS-127A LOROP camera, which has a focal length of sixty-six inches, can also be mounted in station two, but RF-4Cs must be specially modified to employ this camera.

Camera station three is for a high-altitude vertical camera. Its window is just forward of the nose landing gear. The small window next to it is for the optical viewfinder.

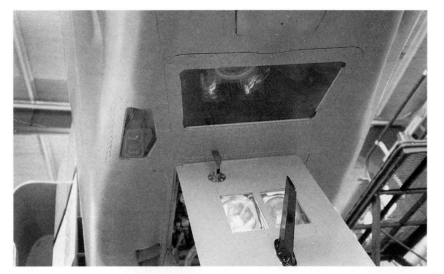

This view looks up into the camera bay at station one. Most of the interior is black or very dark gray.

Looking aft, this photograph shows more details of the inside of the camera bay. The inside of the right side camera window can be seen at the far left.

The camera bay is covered by two doors that open as shown here. Three film cartridges are visible on the ground and are ready for loading into the aircraft.

Details of the inside of the rear camera bay door are illustrated in this photograph.

MODELERS SECTION

KIT REVIEWS

Note: Because the F-4 Phantom is one of the most popular aircraft in aviation history, it is also a favorite among scale modelers. Accordingly, the number of Phantom kits released over the past thirty years is staggering. Although we are only reviewing the kits that represent the F-4C, F-4D, and RF-4C, complete reviews for each issue of these kits would take up far more space than is available in this publication. We have therefore taken two steps to conserve space and still provide all the information necessary for modelers to make informed choices about which model will best suit their needs and desires. First, older kits, which are now of more interest to the collector than the serious scale modeler, are listed with only a few general comments. These kits have been replaced with newer and more accurate releases, and more complete reviews are provided for these more recent kits. Second, most model manufacturers have released and re-released their kits a number of times. In most cases, the later releases are unchanged except for the kit number, box art, and decals. Rather than review every release separately, we are doing a single review to cover all releases of the same basic kit. Where changes have actually been made to the plastic from one release to the next, we are including information about these changes in the reviews. The purpose of this Modelers Section is to help the modeler make the best choice in selecting a model of an F-4C, F-4D, or RF-4C for any specific aircraft he may wish to represent. We have also reviewed a recently-released conversion kit and have briefly discussed some of the accessories that are available for Phantom kits. Lastly, currently available after-market decals are listed. The kits, accessories, and decals are reviewed and listed based on what was available as of December 1993.

Only F-4C, F-4D, and RF-4C kits are reviewed

1/94th SCALE KIT

Lindberg F-4D, Kit Number 489

Released around 1970, this kit is very crude by today's standards, and it is not one that could be considered by the serious scale modeler. It is best left to the collectors, but it is only listed as having a value of about $3.00 in collector's guides.

1/72nd SCALE KITS

Airfix F-4 Phantom Kits, Various Releases

The oldest Phantom kit in 1/72nd scale, the Airfix model was originally released as a Navy F-4B. Over the years, it was subsequently re-released a number of times as F-4C, -D, -E, and -J variants. Although new parts were added to the kit depending on the version represented, the thin F-4B wings and main landing gear remained the same throughout. This meant that the kit did not accurately represent the F-4C, -D, -E, or -J variants. With more up-to-date and accurate 1/72nd scale kits now available for each of these F-4 versions, all of the releases of the Airfix Phantoms are best left to the collectors.

*The 1/72nd scale ESCI/ERTL kit was used to build this model of an F-4C from the Michigan Air National Guard. The aircraft was named **Garfield**, and these markings were chosen because the author flew in this particular aircraft in 1984.*

ESCI F-4C/-J Phantom, Kit Number 9031

Although no longer listed as being commercially available, this kit is still easy to find at swap meets and model contests. It has alternative parts to build an Air Force F-4C or a Navy/Marine F-4J. However, it is also easy to build an F-4D as well.

The parts are molded in silver plastic with separate clear canopy pieces that allow the canopies to be displayed open or closed. Nice engraved lines represent the control surfaces and access panels. However, the fit is relatively poor throughout, and there is a very bad joint between the fuselage and wing.

The cockpits also leave a lot to be desired. There is a big gap between the side consoles and the instrument panels in the rear cockpits. The seats are also poorly represented, so we replaced the ones in our review sample with Verlinden's 1/72nd scale seats. Instruments, switches, and dials are represented by decals for the instrument panels and consoles. There are sink marks on the spine and intake and these must be filled and sanded. For Air Force versions, the holes with the Navy bridle hooks must also be filled and sanded.

Both types of inboard wing pylons are provided, but the ones with the curved leading edge are a little too short in the vertical dimension. Armament consists only of four AIM-7 Sparrow and four AIM-9 Sidewinder missiles. Two 370-gallon tanks and pylons are included for the outboard wing stations, but no armament or fuel tank is provided for the centerline hardpoint. Decals are for a Marine F-4J from VMFA-232 and a Spanish F-4C.

For modelers simply building a model to place on the shelf, this kit is worth considering. However, much better results can be attained by using the Hasegawa or Monogram kits instead.

ESCI RF-4C Phantom, Kit Numbers 9029 and 9121

Using the same basic parts as included in their F-4C/-J kit covered immediately above, ESCI added a few different pieces to create a model of the RF-4C Phantom. These kits also include alternate parts to build an RF-4E.

Issued in 1980, kit 9029 was the first of the two to be released. The same fit problems experienced with the F-4C/-J kit are again present in this kit, but they can be overcome with filling and sanding. The nose section is molded in olive green plastic with individual camera windows molded in clear plastic.

The cockpit arrangement is the same as with the F-4C/-J kit, with decals providing the detailing. In both of these RF-4 releases, the decal for the forward instrument panel is incorrect, being for the fighter version instead of the reconnaissance variants. Again, we recommend replacing the seats with those available from Verlinden. An ALQ-119 ECM pod is provided, and it may be attached to either of the inboard pylons. The outboard wing stations have 370-gallon fuel tanks and pylons attached. There is no tank or pylon provided for the centerline hardpoint. An optional LORAN "towel rack" antenna is included, and it is to be used only if it is appropriate for the particular RF-4C being modeled.

Kit 9121 is identical to 9029 except that it is molded in light gray plastic. Decals in kit 9029 offer the option of building an RF-4C from the Alabama ANG, a Spanish Air Force RF-4C, or a Luftwaffe RF-4E. In kit 9129, markings are provided for two aircraft from the 117th TRW of the Alabama ANG.

Fujimi F-4C/-D Phantoms, Kit Numbers 7A G1, 7A G2, 26103, and 35111

The first issue of this kit was 7A G1, and it consisted of fifty-six parts molded in gray plastic. There were two clear parts, including a one-piece canopy. Kit number 7A G2 was identical, and was the kit used for our review sample. Although the box art and title claim that this kit can be built as an F-4C or F-4D, it only has the F-4C style infrared sensor fairing.

Cockpit detail is quite sparse, and there are large openings between the forward and rear cockpits. The instrument panels are too far forward, and must be repositioned aft. Large gaps exist between the consoles and instrument panels. The control columns must be cut down in height. The ejection seats also leave a lot to be desired, and we recommend replacing them with the Verlinden seats which are covered in the section on accessories below. Decals provide the details for the instrument panels and control columns.

The shape and outline of the model itself is quite good, and details are nicely represented with engraved lines. Fit is generally good except where the underside of the forward wing section meets the fuselage and around the "plugs" that fill in the holes where the Navy bridle hooks would go.

External stores include four Sidewinder and four Sparrow missiles. Additionally, an ALQ-119 ECM pod, a 600-gallon centerline tank, and two 370-gallon wing tanks are provided. Chaff-flare dispensers for the inboard pylons and a LORAN "towel rack" antenna are included as options. A nice feature is that two outboard pylons and a centerline pylon are also included. These can be used on this kit or other 1/72nd scale Phantoms with ordnance attached. The three fuel tanks each have their own pylons molded with the tank, so these separate pylons are extra. In kit 7A G2, decals are provided for Steve Ritchie's famous F-4D, 66-7463, as it appeared while in service with the 18th TFW. Alternative markings are provided for an F-4C from the Hawaii ANG.

Fujimi improved this kit with the issue of kit number 26103. While many of the cockpit problems remain, extra parts are provided to fill the holes between the two cockpits and aft of the rear seat. But the instrument panels still need to be repositioned, the control columns

The Fujimi 1/72nd scale F-4C/-D kit was used to build this model of a triple MiG killer from the Oregon Air National Guard. Decals are from Repli-Scale's excellent sheet of MiG killer Phantoms.

need to be cut down, and the seats need to be replaced. Metal wheels and rubber tires are provided in this new issue, and the canopy is remolded as separate pieces so that it can be displayed in the open position. The fairing for the infrared sensor is updated to look like the one for F-4Ds with the AN/ALR-69(V)-2 modification, but only the "bump" is provided. The small nodes on the "bump" and the forward end of the fairing are missing. The decal sheet includes markings for the 30th Anniversary paint scheme as used by the 906th TFG. Only the **London International Air Show** nose art is provided, while the **Dayton Air And Trade Show** is not. The number that belongs on the nose gear door is also missing. These markings are not as good as those provided on Repli-Scale sheet 72-1010, so we recommend using that sheet if this Phantom is to be modeled. Alternative markings are provided for a MiG killer F-4C from the Oregon ANG and a MiG killer F-4D from the 419th TFW.

A later release of this kit was kit number 35111. It was the same as 26103, except that the decal sheet provided markings for the overall blue F-4D from the North Dakota ANG that was painted in special markings for North Dakota's centennial celebration. Alternative markings were likewise included for several Michigan ANG F-4Cs. This issue can be identified by a sticker that states that markings are provided for the North Dakota centennial aircraft.

Fujimi RF-4C, Kit Number 7A G-14

Like ESCI, Fujimi took its basic F-4C/-D kit and added extra parts to make an RF-4C. This kit is similar to the last two releases of the F-4C/-D kit covered immediately above in that it has the multi-piece canopy and the extra pieces for the cockpit that fill the gaps behind the rear seat and between the two cockpits. But again, the control columns must be shortened, the instrument panels must be repositioned, and the seats need to be replaced.

A nice feature of this kit is that the underside of the reconnaissance nose section is all one piece of clear plastic. It can be attached to the gray pieces which form the rest of the nose section, and the seams can all be filled and sanded without scratching the camera windows. When the model is ready to paint, the modeler just masks off the windows and paints the rest of the nose. Only the two side windows are separate pieces which must be assembled and painted in the conventional manner.

The Sparrow and Sidewinder missiles from the F-4C/-

D kits are retained in this kit, but should not be used. Although a few RF-4Cs were fitted and wired to fire the Sidewinder missile near the end of their service life, they only carried the AIM-9L/-M variants of the missile, and the ones in the kit do not represent these versions. Fuel tanks are provided for the outboard wing and centerline stations, and an ALQ-119 ECM pod is also included in the kit. Decals are for an RF-4C from the Nevada ANG and four aircraft from the 15th TRS of the 18th TRW. One of these four has special markings on the tail used during the reconnaissance meet Photo Finish 1985.

Hasegawa F-4C Phantom, Kit Number KA4 and F-4D Phantom, Kit Number KA5

Hasegawa's line of 1/72nd scale Phantoms are the best F-4 kits in this, the most popular of all modeling scales. Only the Monogram 1/72nd scale Phantoms come close to equaling Has-egawa's excellent models. They are accurate, well detailed, and have the desirable recessed panel lines. The F-4D kit also has the updates made to the actual aircraft including the chaff dispensers on the pylons and the AN/ALR-69(V)-2 modification.

There are only three points where we can fault these kits. The first is that they are overly expensive. While it would be expected that these excellent kits would have a higher price tag than other 1/72nd scale Phantom models, the asking retail price of $25.00 seems excessive when an excellent Monogram 1/72nd scale Phantom is only $9.00. Second, considering the high asking price, the lack of external stores is less than fair in our opinion. The instructions in each of Hasegawa's Phantom kits tell the modeler to get the external stores from the various Hasegawa weapons sets. So after spending a lot of money to get the F-4 kit, the modeler must then invest more money for another Hasegawa kit (or kits) in order to hang weapons, pods, and other stores on his model. While there will always be a need for weapons kits to supplement what comes in the various aircraft kits, we believe that each model should include some basic weapons for the aircraft. The Phantom models do come with

Arguably the best F-4C/-D kit in 1/72nd scale is from Hasegawa. It has engraved panel lines, which are very important to some scale modelers, but it also has a very high price tag. The author used the Hasegawa kit to build this model of an F-4D as it appeared when he flew in it with the 906th TFG at Wright-Patterson Air Force Base. The same aircraft was later painted in the two-tone gray scheme and had special markings applied for the Phantom's thirtieth anniversary. It is illustrated on the front cover of this book.

370-gallon fuel tanks for the outboard wing stations and both types of fuel tanks for the centerline hardpoint. These include the original tank that was designed for the Phantom, and the F-15 style tank that was adopted later in the operational life of the aircraft.

The third area where we would criticize the Hasegawa 1/72nd scale Phantoms is that the cockpit detailing is not very good. The side consoles are parallel to the floor, but they should be angled up slightly. That is to say, the edge nearest the fuselage should be slightly higher than the edge nearest the seat. The ejection seats are pretty good, but they do not have any representation of the seat belts or harness. While these are easily added, they are provided right out of the box in the Monogram kits. Also in the cockpit, the walls of the fuselage are not detailed as they are in the Monogram kits. In fact, the only feature in the cockpits where the Hasegawa kits are better is that they have the gunsight glass represented, while the Monogram kits do not. The Monogram kits have raised detailing on the instrument panels and consoles, while the Hasegawa kits use decals to represent these features. This is really a preference issue, since many modelers may opt for the simpler decals in this scale. Minor negatives include the fact that the ailerons are not drooped and the speed brakes are not opened as they would be when the aircraft is sitting on the ground.

Otherwise, we can offer nothing but praise for the Hasegawa 1/72nd scale Phantoms. Fit is excellent, and all of the parts are molded cleanly with no flash or sink marks. The smallest details, like the blade antennas, the total-temperature probe, and the angle-of-attack probe, are all represented. Shape and outline are accurate, and all of the details are delicate and crisp.

Another plus with these Phantoms is that Hasegawa used one basic kit with part substitutions for other Phantom variants. As a rule, many parts in each kit are not used, because they are intended for other versions. Be sure to save all of these parts. They can be used to improve and update other Phantom kits. Options, such as various ECM antenna fairings, cockpit parts, and wheels are all included so that the model is absolutely accurate.

In kit KA4, decals are provided for the same 57th FIS F-4C as represented in 1/48th scale on Detail & Scale, Sheet number 0148. Alternative markings are also included for F-4Cs from the Oregon and Arkansas Air National Guards. In kit KA5, the kit has markings for the commander's F-4D from the 31st TFW at Homestead AFB, Florida. It is painted in the European 1 scheme and has a ZF tail code and six MiG kills. These were the last markings used operationally on Steve Ritchie's famous 66-7463. Alternative markings are for F-4Ds from the Minnesota and the New York Air National Guard units.

The F-4D kit also has all of the latest modifications made to the aircraft late in its service life. This includes the original infrared sensor fairing and the one with the AN/ALR-69(V)-2 RHAW modification. Chaff dispensers are also included for the inboard pylons, so if a late F-4D is the subject to be modeled, this is the kit to use.

Hasegawa RF-4C, Kit Number KA10

This is the same kit as the two converted immediately above, except that some different parts are included so as

Hasegawa's family of 1/72nd scale Phantoms also includes this model of the RF-4C. This is the best kit that has been released of the RF-4C in any scale to date. Repli-Scale's decals for the commander's aircraft from the 106th TRS were used to represent the Phantom after it returned from Operation Desert Storm.

to produce the RF-4C variant instead of an F-4C or F-4D. Again, this is an excellent kit, and in this case, we believe that it is so much better than the other RF-4C kits in 1/72nd scale, that the high asking price is worth paying.

The Hasegawa kit comes with both the flat and rounded reconnaissance noses, and like the Fujimi kit, the entire underside of the nose is a clear part. The modeler simply chooses which style of nose he wants to use, then glues it to the model. He then fills and sands the minor seam between the gray plastic and the clear part, then paints the nose after masking off the camera windows. Only the side windows must be glued in separately.

All of the appropriate options are provided in this kit to include the correct inboard pylons with the straight leading edge. Fuel tanks and pylons are provided for the outboard wing stations, while both styles of 600-gallon tanks are included for the centerline station. Various blade antennas, bumps, bulges, and other details are optional, leaving the modeler to select exactly what he needs to accurately represent the specific RF-4C he is modeling. Extra parts for the ARN-101 modification on the spine are provided for two of the aircraft represented on the decal sheet. These include RF-4Cs from the 26th TRW and the Alabama ANG in the two tone gray scheme, and a third aircraft from the 18th TFW in the European 1 scheme. We recommend this kit as the best available of the RF-4C in any scale.

Monogram F-4C/-D, Kit Numbers 5439 and 5451

These two kits are exactly the same except for the box art. Both are molded in olive green plastic, and both have a small decal sheet that provides markings for F-4D, 66-7463. Once again, this is the F-4D in which Steve Ritchie scored his first and fifth MiG kills, and it is undoubtedly the most modeled Phantom of all time.

While the Monogram 1/72nd scale Phantom may not be quite as good as the Hasegawa kits, it is still truly excellent, and in some respects it is better. At $9.00, it is certainly the best value among 1/72nd scale Phantoms. What Monogram did was to panagraph down its previously released 1/48th scale F-4C/-D kit, and that is arguably the best kit available of these two versions of the Phantom in any scale. Right out of the box, the kit builds up into a well detailed model. The cockpit is outstanding,

and it features raised detail on the instrument panels, consoles, and the sides of the fuselage. The seat belts and harness are molded on the excellent ejection seats, and all the modeler needs to turn the cockpit into a showpiece is a little paint, skill, and patience. The only item that should be added is the gunsight glass, and this can easily be done from scratch with a small piece of clear plastic and some stretched sprue for framing.

Unlike the Hasegawa kits, this F-4C/-D from Monogram features drooped ailerons and open speed brakes. This is the way the aircraft would appear on the ground. The hydraulic cylinders which operate the speed brakes are molded into the wells rather than extending down to the brakes, but this can be changed if the modeler desires. The landing gear is likewise very well detailed, including the wheel wells and doors.

The Monogram kit does not have the engraved panel lines of the Hasegawa kits, and, although this is important to many modelers, we do not think it is really critical in 1/72nd scale. After placing our finished 1/72nd scale Hasegawa and Monogram models next to each other on a table, both looked equally as good when it came to the representation of panel lines.

The Monogram kit comes with outboard fuel tanks, but none for the centerline station. Instead, a SUU-16 gun pod is supplied for the aircraft's centerline. Four Sparrow and four Sidewinder missiles complete the armament. Additionally, ALQ-87 and ALQ-101(V)-1 ECM pods and a combat camera are also included. Two canopies come with each kit. One is molded as a single piece and is to be used if the canopy is to be shown in the closed position. The other is in four pieces and is used to display either or both canopies in the open position.

The Monogram kit has a unique design for the assembly of the inlets. The bottom of each inlet is molded as part of the lower wing section, and this makes for a better

Monogram's 1/72nd scale kit is excellent, and it is offered at a reasonable price. The ailerons are drooped as they would be on the actual aircraft when it was on the ground, and the speed brakes can be displayed in the open position. Although the panel lines are raised, they are accurate and well represented. Cockpit and ejection seat details are the best on any 1/72nd scale Phantom. The author built this model to represent the F-4D which is pictured at the top of page 53.

fit on the underside. On other kits there is a bad joint where the underside of the wing meets the forward fuselage, and this area usually requires a lot of filling and sanding. The one bad problem on this kit concerns the inner portion of the inlet ramps. The framework around the tiny holes stands far too proud from the plastic.

The LORAN "towel rack" antenna is provided as an option, but the Monogram kits were designed and released before chaff dispensers were added to the inboard pylons or the AN/ALR-69(V)-2 modification was added to the infrared sensor fairing on F-4Ds. So these features will have to be taken from another kit or added from scratch if a late F-4D is to be built. But for all F-4Cs and over ninety percent of the service life of the F-4D, this Monogram kit is an excellent choice.

Revell F-4C, Various Kit Number H-229

Revell's 1/72nd scale Phantom kit is second only to the Airfix model when it comes to age. Like the Airfix kit, Revell's Phantom was first released as a Navy F-4B. Kit H-229 was a re-release of the same kit as one of Revell's "Jet Commando" series aircraft. Although it was supposed to represent an F-4C, it retained the thin wings and main landing gear which are characteristic of the F-4B. With much better F-4C/-D kits now available, this Revell model has become a collector's item.

Testors RF-4C, Kit Number 682

This model has actually been released twice as kit number 682, but only the decals and box art were changed from one release to the next. The first time the kit was issued, the markings on the decal sheet were for an RF-4C from the 363rd TRW. Optional markings were also included for West German and Japanese RF-4Es. In the more recent release, the decal sheet provided markings for an RF-4C from the 67th TRW and another from the Nevada ANG.

In many respects, this kit is a scaled down version of Testors' 1/48th scale RF-4C, but there are some differences. For example, the vents at the aft end of the fairings that cover the forward Sparrow bays are included in this kit. They were missing from the 1/48th scale kit. But other vents, like those on the tops and bottoms of the

RF-4C/E Phantom II

Includes Parts and Markings for an RF-4C and Extra Parts for an RF-4E

1/72 scale, Unassembled Kit Recommended for Experienced Modelers Ages 10 and Over   *Photograph Not to Scale Actual Length 10¾" (26.2 cm)*   *Paint, Cement, and Hobby Accessories Not Included*

Testors' 1/72nd scale RF-4C/-E is basically a scaled down version of their 1/48th scale kit. It has some inaccuracies and lacks some basic detailing.

inlets, are represented by decals. Another vent, located aft of the nose gear well, is also represented only by a decal. Fuel tanks are provided for the outboard wing stations and the centerline hardpoint, but the centerline tank is the older style designed for the Phantom. The newer style tank can be obtained for a Hasegawa kit or from most F-15 kits.

Although this is not a bad kit, detailing in the cockpit, landing gear, and elsewhere is not as good on this kit as it is on the Hasegawa, Fujimi, or ESCI kits. For this reason, we believe that most serious scale modelers will prefer one of those kits over this one.

1/48th SCALE KITS

ESCI (Scale Craft) F-4C/-D, Kit Number SC-4044

This is an older model of the F-4C/-D, and it was released when Scale Craft was marketing the ESCI line. Although the shape and outline of this kit are good, it is not as well done as the present Monogram and Hasegawa kits. It was derived from the ESCI F-4E kit, and it still has the poorly represented slotted stabilators which are incorrect for an F-4C or F-4D. This is the only kit of the F-4C/-D ever released with recessed panel lines, but these lines were a little heavy by today's standards. This kit is no longer available, so it is best to leave it to the collectors and opt for the Monogram or Hasegawa kits instead.

This ESCI F-4C/-D model is the only 1/48th scale kit of these versions of the Phantom with engraved panel lines. While it is basically a good kit, it does not measure up to the quality and detailing of the Monogram and Hasegawa kits.

Hasegawa F-4C/-D, Kit Number P6

This kit has been released at least twice with the same number. In the first release, the decals provided markings for F-4C, 63-7647, from the Hawaii ANG. Two additional sets of markings were also provided for Steve Ritchie's famous F-4D, 66-7463. In one case the markings were for the aircraft at the time Ritchie flew it with the 555th TFS of the 432nd TRW. At that time the aircraft had the OY tail code and five kills were displayed on its left inlet ramp. The second option was for the aircraft as it appeared in later service with the 44th TFS of the 18th TFW. The tail code had been changed to ZZ, and six MiG kills were on the inlet ramp. In the second release, the decal sheet had markings for four F-4Cs from the Michigan ANG. Other markings were included for an

F-4C from the Hawaii ANG and an F-4D from the Alabama ANG. It should be noted that the tail markings provided for the F-4D from the Alabama ANG were black. They should have been Gunship Gray, FS 36118.

Very little change was made to the plastic between the two releases. In the second issue, the AN/ALR-69(V)-2 modification was added to the infrared sensor fairing beneath the radome, and chaff dispensers were provided for the inboard pylons. So this is the kit to choose if the aircraft to be represented is an F-4D late in its service life.

Unlike the Hasegawa 1/72nd scale F-4C/-D, this kit does not have recessed panel lines. The ailerons are not drooped as they should be if the aircraft was sitting on the ground. However, the speed brakes are separate pieces, and the actuating cylinders are also separate.

In our review of Hasegawa's 1/72nd scale F-4C, F-4D, and RF-4C Phanotms, we listed three major criticisms, but only two of them apply to this 1/48th scale release. This is because four AIM-7 Sparrows and four AIM-9 Sidewinders are included, so some basic armament comes with this kit. But the other two criticisms are valid for this 1/48th scale kit as well as for Hasegawa's 1/72nd scale Phantoms. First, the $37.50 retail price seems excessive to us. While we would expect this kits to cost more than the Monogram 1/48th scale Phantoms, why should it be over three times as much? Since the Hasegawa 1/48th scale F-4C/-D kit does not offer the advantage of engraved panel lines, and it is inferior to the Monogram kits in certain important respects, modelers may want to seriously consider the value received for the dollars spent when it comes to choosing which 1/48th scale F-4C/-D kit to buy.

The second major criticism of the Hasegawa 1/48th scale F-4C/-D kit is that the cockpit detailing leaves something to be desired. The side consoles in the rear cockpit are parallel to the floor, while they should be angled up slightly. The edge nearest the fuselage should be higher than the edge nearest the seat. Instruments, knobs, and switches on the instrument panels and consoles are represented with raised detailing, but this is not accurate for any cockpit we have seen in an F-4C or F-4D. A small amount of detailing is on the fuselage sides, but

this is not as extensive nor as accurate as what is provided in the Monogram kit. The area behind the rear seat also is not correctly detailed as it is on the Monogram kit. The ejection seats are good, but they lack any representation of the seat belts or harness. Since the kit includes pilot and WSO figures, Hasegawa must have thought that this was not important, but few modelers include crew figures in their models. The belts and harness are easily added, but it would be nice to have these included in the box, especially considering its high price tag.

In all other respects, the kit is quite good. It is very well detailed, and it has crisp molding and delicate parts. The clear canopy pieces are thin and well formed. An angle-of-attach probe is represented on both sides of the nose. The one on the right side is incorrect and should be removed. The total-temperature probe is not included in the kit, and this is surprising, because it is in Hasegawa's 1/72nd scale kits. Both types of 600-gallon centerline tanks are provided as are 370-gallon tanks for the outboard wing stations. Additionally, separate pylons are included for the outboard and centerline hardpoints, and ordnance from the Hasegawa 1/48th scale weapons sets or other kits may be attached to them.

This is unquestionably a very good kit, but considering its high price, we would have expected far better cockpit detailing. But it is also the most up-to-date F-4C/-D model in 1/48th scale. Each modeler will have to decide whether it is worth the price.

Monogram F-4C/-D. Kit Numbers 5800, 5821, and 5831

We rate these Monogram kits as the best F-4C/-D kits in 1/48th scale. Ranging from $11.25 for kits 5800 and 5821, to $14.50 for the "high-tech" 5831, there is no question that these are the best kits as far as value is concerned, but we also consider them simply to be the best irrespective of price.

The original issue was kit 5800, and it had markings for COL Robin Olds' F-4C, 63-7680, from the 8th TFW. Alternate markings were included for Steve Ritchie's F-4D, 66-7463, and for an F-4D, 66-8793, from the 52nd TFW. Kit 5821 had a decal sheet that provided markings

Hasegawa's 1/48th scale F-4C/-D has been released twice, and the kit with this box art represents the F-4D with the last modifications the aircraft received while still in service. It is an excellent kit but does not have the engraved panel lines of Hasegawa's 1/72nd scale Phantom.

The 1/48th scale F-4C/-D kit from Monogram is very accurate and well detailed. Although it does not have some of the last modifications made to the aircraft while it was in service, it is an accurate model of the F-4C and F-4D during most of their service life. It has a better detailed and more accurate cockpit than the Hasegawa kit and is available at a much more reasonable price.

for an F-4C, 64-860, from the New York ANG. Kit 5831 had markings for F-4C, 63-7411, when it served with the Arkansas ANG. At the time it was the oldest Phantom operational in TAC. Special nose art denoted this fact. Detailing is excellent throughout. The cockpit is superb, lacking only the gunsight glass which is easy to add from clear plastic and stretched sprue. All of the details on the instrument panels, consoles, and fuselage sides are accurate and complete. The ejection seats include the belts and harnesses. Right out of the box, the modeler can produce an outstanding cockpit. Detailing for the landing gear is likewise very good. The ailerons are in the drooped position, and the speed brakes are separate so that they can be shown open. We would have preferred to have the actuating cylinders for the brakes as separate pieces instead of having them molded into the wells.

Surface scribing is raised, but is nicely done and quite accurate. We rate it better than what is in the Hasegawa kit. The one flaw is on the inlet ramps where the framing around the tiny holes stands too proud. Monogram must have realized this error, because in their "high tech" kit number 5831, perforated metal plates are provided to go over these two ramps. Also in kit 5831, photoetched metal parts are provided to further detail the ejection seats and the interior of the afterburner cans. Small mirrors and hooks are also included for the canopy rails.

Armament consists of four Sidewinders, four Sparrows, and one SUU-16 gun pod. ALQ-87 and ALQ-101(V)-1 ECM pods are also provided as is a combat camera. Two 370-gallon fuel tanks are supplied for the outboard wing stations. One shortcoming of these kits is that they don't have the chaff dispensers for the inboard pylons nor the AN/ALR-69(V)-2 modification to the infrared sensor that were added late in the operational service of the F-4D. But otherwise, these are excellent kits, and we recommend them as the best available of the F-4C/-D.

Testors RF-4C, Kit Number 582

This is the first, and so far the only, reconnaissance Phantom available in 1/48th scale. It has been issued as an RF-4B, RF-4C, and RF-4E. Decals for the RF-4C were for an aircraft from the 363rd TRW.

The outline and shape of this kit is generally accurate. Detailing of the landing gear is good, and the fit of the parts is about average. Some filling and sanding is required, but there are no serious problem areas. Raised scribing represents the various panels on the skin of the

The only 1/48th scale RF-4C version of the Phantom that has been released to date is from Testors. It suffers from poor cockpit detailing and lacks some important details. However, it is generally a good kit, and it can be built into a very attractive model with a little work.

aircraft, and this leaves a bit to be desired. Most modelers will want to sand this off and rescribe the various surfaces. While doing so, be sure to add the vents on the tops and bottoms of the inlets, since Testors chose to represent these with decals. The vents at the aft end of the fairings which cover the forward Sparrow bays and another vent between these fairings are likewise missing. These should be scribed into the plastic as well. Adding these vents is not too difficult and does not require much time, but it will add a lot to the appearance of the model.

The major deficiency with the model is in the cockpit area. There are gaps between the consoles and the cockpit sides and behind both seats where you can see all the way down to the bottom of the fuselage. There is also a gap in front of the rear instrument panel and gaps between the side consoles and the instrument panels where the auxiliary panels should be. All of this can be corrected with thin sheet plastic. Two instrument panels are provided for the front cockpit, but the instructions tell you to use the wrong one. The one which is wider at the top is the correct one to use. The seats are poor, and should be replaced with scratchbuilt seats or ones from Verlinden. One modeler we know simply used the cockpit parts from a Monogram 1/48th scale kit to solve all of these problems. He said he only had to make a few easy adjustments in fit, and he modified the forward instrument panel to look like one in an RF-4C.

The kit provides two 370-gallon fuel tanks for the outboard wing stations, and the original style 600-gallon tank is included for the centerline hardpoint. Be sure to use the inboard pylons with the straight leading edge. These the correct ones to use, and the optional pylons with the curved leading edge are the wrong shape.

While this kit does not measure up to the Hasegawa and Monogram F-4C/-D kits, it can be built up into an excellent model with a little time and patience. By using parts from a Monogram 1/48th scale F-4C/-D to correct some of the problems, it can be improved considerably. This approach will cost less money and take less time than doing a conversion. Unfortunately, neither Monogram nor Hasegawa have yet modified their 1/48th scale F-4C/-D kits to the RF-4C configuration. Until they do, this is the best way to build an RF-4C in this scale.

UPC (Entex) F-4C, Various Kit Numbers

This was the first F-4C kit in 1/48th scale, and it has been issued by several manufacturers. It was really a toy with a variety of working features instead of a scale model. It cannot be considered by the serious modeler and should be left to the collectors---or kids!

1/32nd SCALE KITS

To date, no kits have been released of the F-4C, F-4D, or RF-4C in 1/32nd scale. Revell did issue an RF-4B in this scale, and with a lot of work it could be built into a representation of the RF-4C. Revell's F-4J in 1/32nd scale could, with even more work, be converted to an F-4C or an F-4D. But the Revell 1/32nd scale Phantom kits are old, have a lot of shape and fit problems, and generally are not of high enough quality to be considered by the serious modeler. We have seen one of Revell's F-4E kits turned into a fine model with over 2500 hours of work, but because of the inaccuracies in shape and outline, these kits are not recommended.

But help should be coming soon. Tamiya, who has just released an outstanding F-15E Strike Eagle in 1/32nd scale, has announced that a 1/32nd scale Phantom is on the way. As of this writing, it is not known which version of the Phantom will be represented, but any variant would be welcomed. We are hoping that Tamiya will design their molds so that several variants can and will be released. If they are anything like the F-15E Strike Eagle kit, they will be the answer to a lot of modelers' prayers.

CONVERSION KIT

<u>HighFlight Replicas 1/48th Scale RF-4 Conversion Kit Number 4808</u>

Although Testors has marketed 1/48th scale RF-4B and RF-4Cs kits for many years, HighFlight Replicas has released a resin kit to convert the Hasegawa F-4B/-N models to an RF-4B and the Hasegawa F-4C/-D kits to an RF-4C. The title on the box says, "RF-4B Photo Phantom, Seen in Desert Storm." Actually, the RF-4B was not used in Desert Storm, but the RF-4C was. A photograph of a completed RF-4C model in the markings of the 106th TRS is used as the box art.

While the Hasegawa kits are better than the Testors kit, we are not really sure why a modeler would choose to pay the extra dollars and do the additional work required by this conversion. First, the Hasegawa F-4C and F-4D kits do not have the more desirable engraved panel lines, so this reason is out. Second, this is almost an exact copy of the Testors nose section as far as shape and outline go, and HighFlight, like Testors, left off the vents at the aft end of the fairings that cover the forward missile bays. Third, the Testors kit, although it has some problems, is not really that bad, and it can be built into an excellent model with less work than this conversion. It seems to us that the better alternative is to improve the Testors kit rather than to do the conversion, but this is something each modeler must decide.

This HighFlight kit has two large resin pieces for the

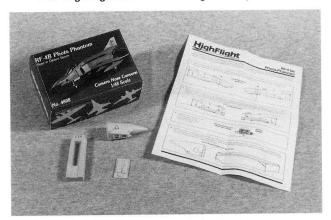

High Flight has released this 1/48th scale kit for converting a Hasegawa F-4C/-D to an RF-4B/-C. However, the kit is missing several vents on the underside of the aircraft, and it does not provide the clear parts for the windows.

nose section and the area around the nose landing gear. A smaller third part is actually a flat piece of resin with a small modification for the forward instrument panel and the two covers for the forward Sparrow missiles bays molded into it. Surprisingly, there are no clear parts provided for the camera windows. Instead, the modeler is left to cut his own windows out of clear sheet plastic. A camera is molded into each side window, and while this configuration is technically possible, the standard configuration in camera station two would be a single camera which is rotated from side to side as required.

Step five on the instruction sheet says to, "Fill and sand smooth both missile bays." As a point of clarification, this must mean the rear two bays, because parts are provided to go over the forward bays. The instructions do not tell the modeler to remove the pitot probe from the vertical tail, but this must be done for the RF-4B/-C. The instructions also fail to tell the modeler to change the inboard pylons to the type which have the straight leading edge for the RF-4C. The ones that come in the Hasegawa F-4C/-D kits have the curved leading edge. Any RHAW antenna fairings at the top of the trailing edge of the vertical tail must also be removed, and the instructions likewise fail to mention this.

For modelers who simply like doing conversions and working with resin parts, this kit can be used to build a nice RF-4C. But we believe that most modelers will be more than satisfied with the results that can be attained simply by improving and detailing the Testors kit.

F-4 MODEL ACCESSORIES

Over the years a number of companies have manufactured accessories to help modelers improve existing F-4 Phantom kits. These range from simple instrument panel placards to an extensive detailing set. The following is a listing of some of these accessories that are readily available and which are worth considering by the serious scale modeler.

Airwaves and Photo Cut both make photoetched metal detail sets for Phantom canopies in 1/72nd and 1/48th scales. Although they are a little harder to find, similar sets are available from Model Technologies which also produced a set in 1/32nd scale as well. In addition to their canopy detail set, Airwaves also has a photo-etched metal F-4 Phantom cockpit detail set and a seat belt set. Both the cockpit detail set and the seat belt set are available in 1/72nd and 1/48th scales.

Airkit, also marketed as "plus model," offers 1/72nd scale cockpit placards printed on thin clear plastic for the F-4C, F-4D, and RF-4C. True Details has released bulged and flattened tires for the Phantom in 1/72nd scale. HighFlight makes afterburner cans and nozzles in 1/72nd and 1/48th scales, and Benchwork has a nice kit in 1/48th scale that allows the modeler to add detailed inlet interiors and afterburner cans to his model.

Koster Aero Enterprises makes a vacuformed kit that includes intake covers to fit several Monogram models in 1/48th scale. Included among these covers are a pair for the F-4 Phantom. With some minor sanding and filing, these can also be made to fit the 1/48th scale Hasegawa

Many detailing parts are available for the F-4 from a number of companies. Four examples are shown here. At top left are bulged and flattened tires from True Details. Model Technologies is only one of several companies that have produced photoetched metal parts for canopies and cockpits as seen at top right. Verlinden's 1/72nd scale ejection seats are shown at bottom left, and are also available in 1/48th scale. HighFlight produces the afterburner cans and nozzles seen in the lower right corner of the photograph.

kits as well. For more information about Koster's products, send a self-addressed, stamped envelope to; Koster Aero Enterprises, 25 Glenridge Drive, Bedford, MA 01730.

Verlinden makes excellent ejection seats for the F-4 in both 1/72nd and 1/48th scales. For the serious detailer, Verlinden also offers a resin and photoetched brass detail kit for the Phantom in 1/72nd scale. A 1/48th scale kit is also available, but it is designed for the F-4E variant.

DECAL LISTING

Note: Many after-market decal sheets for the F-4 Phantom have been released over the years. Most of these are still available commercially, but some can be found only on collector's tables at swap meets or model contests. Others are now very difficult if not impossible to find. The following is a list of after-market decal sheets that provide markings for the F-4C, F-4D, and RF-4C that are commercially available as of December 1993, or which the modeler may have a reasonable likelihood of finding at a model contest or swap meet. For the most part, this is only a listing of decals, but a few comments relating to accuracy have been made when we have used a given decal sheet and found a problem.

1/144th SCALE

It should be noted that there are no kits presently available of the F-4C, F-4D, or RF-4C in 1/144th scale.

Super Scale (formerly Microscale), Sheet Number 14-76
This sheet provides markings for the same aircraft as listed below for Super Scale sheet number 72-076.

1/72nd SCALE

Aerodecal, Sheet Number 25A
Markings for F-4C, F-4D, F-4E, and RF-4C Phantoms that were assigned to units in USAFE are provided on this sheet. All aircraft are in the standard camouflage scheme. The F-4C, F-4D, and RF-4C aircraft and their assigned units are as follows:
F-4C, 63-7467, 52nd TFW, 81st TFS
F-4D, 66-8720, 36th TFW, 53rd TFS
F-4D, 65-703, 50th TFW, 10th TFS
F-4D, 66-8765, 48th TFW
F-4D, 66-232, 81st TFW, 92nd TFS (misidentified as 64-232)
RF-4C, 69-374, 26th TRW, 38th TRS
RF-4C, 64-1019, 10th TRW, 30th TRS

ESCI, Sheet Number 88
This sheet includes markings for six F-4B, -C, -D, -E, and -K Phantoms. The decals have very heavy yellow film. The F-4C and the F-4D are in the standard camouflage scheme and are for the following aircraft:
F-4C, 63-7633, 347th TFW, 35th TFS
F-4D, 64-1019, 306th FS, Imperial Iranian Air Force

Modeldecal, Sheet Number 2
Markings for three Phantoms, including one F-4C, are provided on this sheet. The F-4C is 63-7663, and it is represented at the time it was assigned to the 8th TFW, 555th TFS, and flown by COL Robin Olds.

Repli-Scale, Sheet Number 72-1007
Two F-4Cs from the Oregon Air National Guard are the subjects on this sheet. However, these are misidentified as F-4Ds on the instruction sheet.
F-4C, 63-7704, in the European 1 scheme
F-4C, 63-7490, in the two-tone gray scheme

Repli-Scale, Sheet Number 72-1010
This sheet provides markings for F-4D, 66-765. The aircraft is from the 906th TFG and is in the two-tone gray camouflage scheme with special markings for the 30th anniversary of the F-4 Phantom. Nose art includes **London International Air Show**, but not the later **Dayton Air and Trade Show**. The number for the forward nose gear door is missing, otherwise this is an excellent sheet.

Repli-Scale, Sheet Number 72-1028
On this excellent sheet, four F-4C MiG killers from the Vietnam War are represented as they appeared in later service with the Air National Guard. Each aircraft has a different paint scheme and a different number of kills.
F-4C, 63-7704, one MiG kill, special gray camouflage scheme, Louisiana ANG
F-4C, 64-829, two MiG kills, wraparound scheme, Texas ANG
F-4C, 64-776, three MiG kills, (plus two drone kills from William Tell, 1984), ADC gray scheme, Oregon ANG

F-4C, 64-806, four MiG kills, standard camouflage scheme, Hawaii ANG

Repli-Scale, Sheet Number 72-1031

This sheet provides markings for four RF-4Cs and two RF-4B Phantoms. The RF-4Cs are painted in the two-tone gray scheme and are as follows:

RF-4C, 65-854, CO's aircraft, 117th TRW, BH tail code, special markings on inlets

RF-4C, 65-853. CO's aircraft 106th TRS, BH tail code, sharksmouth and Desert Storm mission markings

RF-4C, 64-1044, 117th TRW, BH tail code

RF-4C. 64-1043, 117th TRW, BH tail code, named **Smooth Character**

The gray for the serial numbers for 65-854 and 65-853 are too light. They should be FS 36118. These can easily be replaced with numbers from another decal sheet which provides dark gray numbers.

Super Scale, Sheet Number 72-076

Markings for four F-4Cs and two F-4Es are provided on this sheet of Vietnam era Phantoms. The F-4Cs are from the 12th TFW and are painted in the standard camouflage scheme. They are as follows:

F-4C, 64-665, 557th TFS, XC tail code, named **HELL'S ANGEL.**

F-4C, 63-7413, 559th TFS, XN tail code, named **BLUE AVENGER**

F-4C, 63-7522, 556th TFS, XT tail code, named **SAINTLY SINNER**

F-4C, 63-7604, 559th TFS, XN tail code, named **SUGAR FOOT III**

Super Scale, Sheet Number 72-112

Several different types of Phantoms can be modeled using this sheet which includes markings for two RF-4Cs, one F-4C, and three F-4Es in the standard camouflage scheme. The RF-4Cs and F-4C are as follows:

RF-4C, 64-1033, 432nd TRW, 11th TRS, OO tail code, named **OL Bullet**

RF-4C, 65-870, 432nd TRW, OO tail code, named **Hillbilly Slick** (misidentified on sheet as an F-4C)

F-4C, 64-829, 8th TFW, 555th TFS, FG tail code, named **SCAT XXVII**, two MiG kills, flown by COL Robin Olds

Super Scale, Sheet Number 72-137

This sheet provides markings for Phantoms in fancy markings, one of which is the YF-4C prototype in special markings used at Edwards Air Force Base.

Super Scale, Sheet Number 72-144

Markings for several MiG killer Phantoms are on this sheet. Two of these are the following F-4Ds which are painted in the standard camouflage scheme:

F-4D, 66-7463, 555th TFS, OY tail code, flown by Steve Ritchie for his first and fifth kills

F-4D, 66-7554, 555th TFS, OY tail code, named **Trapper**, with Snoopy painted on left air inlet.

Super Scale, Sheet Number 72-164

This sheet provides Phantom stenciling in black.

Super Scale, Sheet Number 72-198

A large number of Phantom markings are provided on this sheet including eight F-4Es, two F-4Cs, and two F-4Ds. The F-4Cs and F-4Ds are painted in the standard camouflage scheme and include:

F-4C, 64-937, North Dakota ANG (The sheet says this is an F-4D, but the serial number is for an F-4C.)

F-4C, 63-7460, 57th FIS (The sheet says this is an F-4D, but it is an F-4C. The markings are very inaccurate.)

F-4D, 66-7649, 49th TFW commander's aircraft

F-4D, 66-8793, 52nd TFW, 23rd TFS

Super Scale, Sheet Number 72-224

This sheet has markings for two F-4Es and two F-4Cs. The F-4Cs are both in the standard camouflage scheme and are for the following aircraft:

F-4C, 63-7584, 58th TFTW commander's aircraft with black and white high visibility stripes

F-4C, 63-7676, 58th TFTW, bi-centennial markings

Super Scale, Sheet Number 72-237

This sheet provides Phantom stenciling in white.

Super Scale, Sheet Number 72-293

Called "USAF Gray Phantoms," since all of the aircraft are painted in the ADC Gray scheme, this sheet provides markings for one F-4E and three F-4Cs. The F-4Cs are as follows:

F-4C, 64-937, North Dakota Air National Guard

F-4C, 64-785, Hawaii Air National Guard

F-4C, 63-7618, Michigan Air National Guard

Super Scale, Sheet Number 72-320

All of the Phantoms represented on this sheet are reconnaissance variants to include one RF-4B and three RF-4Cs. The RF-4Cs are painted in the standard camouflage scheme and are marked as follows:

RF-4C, 64-1009, 363rd TRW, JO tail code

RF-4C, 66-423, Kentucky ANG, KE tail code

RF-4C, 68-571, 26th TRW, ROYAL FLUSH '74

Super Scale, Sheet Number 72-324

More recon Phantoms are on this sheet to include markings for two RF-4Bs and three RF-4Cs. The RF-4Cs are in the standard camouflage scheme and include the following:

RF-4C, 63-7753, CO's aircraft, TRC

RF-4C, 65-905, 11th TRS, OO tail code

RF-4C, 63-7753, Alabama ANG, USA on tail (**Montgomery** and the stripes on the red tail band should be gold, not white.)

Super Scale, Sheet Number 72-369

Markings for four additional RF-4Cs are provided on this sheet. Included are:

RF-4C, 65-897, Nevada ANG, wraparound camouflage, in markings for PHOTO FINISH '81

RF-4C, 64-1063, Kentucky ANG, wraparound scheme

RF-4C, 64-1050, Nebraska ANG, wraparound scheme

RF-4C, 65-828, Nebraska ANG, standard camouflage

Super Scale, Sheet Number 72-371

This sheet has markings for two F-4Es and Two F-

4Ds. The F-4Ds are both in the standard camouflage scheme, and the markings are for the following aircraft:

F-4D, 65-731, 31st TFW, CO's aircraft, ZF tail code
F-4D, 66-7678, 4th TFW, CO's aircraft, SA tail code, flown by COL Chuck Yeager

Super Scale, Sheet Number 72-380

Three F-4Cs are represented on this sheet as follows:
F-4C, 64-829, 915th TFG, 93rd TFS, AFRES, FM tail code, standard camouflage scheme, two MiG kills
F-4C, 64-776, Oregon ANG, standard camouflage scheme, three MiG kills
F-4C, 64-776, Oregon ANG, same aircraft as above in ADC Gray scheme

Super Scale, Sheet Number 72-385

Two F-4Es and one F-4C are included on this sheet. The F-4C is 63-7589 and is from the 36th TFS of the 3rd TFW. It is in the standard camouflage scheme, and has a UK tail code. A MiG kill marking is on the inlet ramp.

Super Scale, Sheet Number 72-468

This sheet provides markings for two F-4Cs and two F-4Ds.
F-4C, 63-7704, Louisiana ANG, one MiG kill, special two tone gray camouflage scheme
F-4C, 64-841, Louisiana ANG, special two tone gray camouflage scheme but different from aircraft above
F-4D, 66-7466, Minnesota ANG, ADC Gray scheme
F-4D, 66-7745, Alabama ANG, European 1 scheme

Super Scale, Sheet Number 72-492

Markings for two F-4Cs and one F-4D are included on this sheet.
F-4C, 63-7583, Michigan ANG, ADC Gray scheme, named **Garfield** or **Never Trust A Smiling Cat**
F-4C, 63-7702, Texas ANG, ADC Gray scheme
F-4D, 66-7554, 906th TFG, 89th TFS, European 1 scheme with two MiG kills, named **City of Fairborn**

Super Scale, Sheet Number 72-541

This sheet has markings for two Marine F-4S Phantoms and one F-4D. The F-4D is 66-7681 and is from the Alabama ANG. It has an AL tail code and is painted in the two-tone gray scheme. However, these decals are unusable. The gray used for the markings that go over the lighter gray on the aircraft are so light that they cannot be seen when they are applied. These markings should be FS 36118, but they are almost the same shade as the lighter FS 36440 gray to which they are to be applied.

Super Scale, Sheet Number 72-659

Three RF-4Cs in the two-tone gray scheme are the subjects for this sheet. These are:
RF-4C, 65-870, Nevada ANG
RF-4C, 69-370, 26th TRW, 38th TRS, ZR tail code
RF-4C, 69-357, 67th RW CO's aircraft, BA tail code

1/48th SCALE SHEETS

Aerodecal, Sheet Number 27C

This is the same as Aerodecal, sheet number 25A which is covered above, except that it is in 1/48th scale.

Bare Metal (now Experts Choice), Sheet Number 4

Three F-4Cs from the Michigan Air National Guard are on this sheet. It is an old release which has now been replaced with sheet number 48-32 listed below.
F-4C, 63-7534, named **DEFIANCE II**, ADC Gray scheme
F-4C, 63-7529, no name, ADC Gray scheme
F-4C, 63-7626, no name, standard camouflage

Detail & Scale, Sheet Number 0148

This sheet provides markings for three F-4Cs.
F-4C, 63-7618, 57th FIS, in the standard camouflage with bi-centennial and William Tell markings
F-4C, 63-7576, commander's aircraft from the Air Defense Weapon's Center in the ADC Gray scheme
F-4C, 64-785, Hawaii ANG in the ADC Gray scheme

Detail & Scale, Sheet Number 0248

Markings for three wing commander's F-4Ds are provided on this sheet. All are painted in the standard camouflage scheme.
F-4D, 65-731, 31st TFW CO's aircraft, ZF tail code
F-4D, 64-949, 49th TFW CO's aircraft, HO tail code
F-4D, 65-756, 56th TFW CO's aircraft, MC tail code

Experts Choice, Sheet Number 48-9

F-4Ds from the Minnesota ANG are represented on this sheet, and all are painted in the ADC Gray scheme. Crew names and rows of numbers are included to allow the modeler to build a variety of aircraft from this unit.

Experts Choice, Sheet Number 48-11

This sheet provides markings for F-4Cs from the Texas ANG in the ADC Gray scheme. Various crew names and rows of numbers are included to allow the modeler to build a variety of aircraft from this unit.

Experts Choice, Sheet Number 48-32

F-4Cs from the Michigan Air National Guard, each painted in the ADC Gray scheme with special nose art, make this an interesting sheet. Included are:
63-7534, named **DEFIANCE II**
63-7626, named **No More Mr. Nice Guy**
63-7576, named **Never Give A Sucker an Even Break**
63-7595, named **Make My Day**
63-7442, named **Shadow Demon**
63-7666, named **This One's For You Baby**
63-7412, named **We Bad**
63-7475, named **Defender of Freedom**
63-7583, named **Garfield** or **Never Trust a Smiling Cat**
63-7618, named **Double Trouble**

Experts Choice, Sheet Number 48-40

Like sheet number 48-32 listed immediately above, this sheet provides additional markings for F-4Cs from the Michigan Air National Guard in the ADC Gray scheme with special nose art. The aircraft include the following:
63-7529, named **Trussst Me**
63-7460, named **Puff the Magic Dragon**
63-7482, named **Patience My Ass**

63-7536, named **Cirano The Fearless**
63-7475, named **Swine Trek**
64-707, named **I Don't Take Defeat Lightly**
63-7442, named **Baby**
64-707, named **Don't Mess With The Kid**
63-7666, named **I Don't Get Mad, I Get Even**

Fowler (No Sheet Number)

This sheet has markings for two F-4Cs.

F-4C, 63-7664, in the early light gull gray over white scheme, TAC insignia and lightning bolt on tail

F-4C, 63-7589, Michigan Air National Guard aircraft in the ADC Gray scheme. The **Michigan** on the tail is the wrong style and is too small.

Repli-Scale, Sheet Number 48-5010

This sheet provides the same markings as sheet number 72-1010 covered above in the 1/72nd scale listings. The same comments apply to this 1/48th scale sheet.

Repli-Scale, Sheet Number 48-5028

This is the 1/48th scale version of sheet 72-1028 covered above in the 1/72nd scale listings.

Repli-Scale, Sheet Number 48-5031

This is the same as sheet 72-1031 covered above.

IPMS/USA, No Sheet Number

This limited edition sheet provided markings for thirteen USAF and German F-4s. Included were the following F-4Cs and F-4Ds:

F-4C, 63-7442, Michigan ANG, named **Shadow Demon**, in the ADC Gray scheme

F-4C, 63-7460, Michigan ANG, named **Puff the Magic Dragon**, in the ADC Gray scheme

F-4C, 63-7482, Michigan ANG, named **Patience My Ass**, in the ADC Gray scheme

F-4C, 63-7529, Michigan ANG, named **Trussst Me**, in the ADC scheme

F-4C, 63-7589, 57th FIS, in the ADC Gray scheme with one MiG kill

F-4C, 64-829, 8th TFW, named **SCAT**, FG tail code, standard camouflage scheme, flown by COL Robin Olds, two MiG kills

F-4D, 66-7764, 8th TFW, 435th TFS, FO tail code, standard camouflage scheme

F-4D, 66-239, 8th TFW, 497th TFS, FP tail code, standard camouflage scheme, The sheet misidentifies this as 68-239, but this is not a valid number for an F-4D.

Super Scale, Sheet Number 48-034

This sheet has markings for a Marine F-4J and a USAF F-4C. The F-4C is 63-7676, and it has bi-centennial markings used by the 58th TFTW at Luke AFB. It is painted in the standard camouflage scheme.

Super Scale, Sheet Number 48-046

Markings for two Navy F-4Bs and one USAF F-4C are provided on this sheet. The F-4C is 63-7584, and it is the commander's aircraft from the 58th TFTW at Luke AFB. It has black and white high visibility stripes and is painted in the standard camouflage scheme.

Super Scale, Sheet Number 48-067

This sheet provides Phantom stenciling in black.

Super Scale, Sheet Number 48-072

This sheet has markings for a Navy F-4J (misidentified on the instructions as an F-4B), one F-4C (misidentified as an F-4D), and an F-4D. The two USAF Phantoms are as follows:

F-4C, 63-7460, 57th FIS, standard camouflage, The markings for this aircraft are very inaccurate.

F-4D, 66-8793, 52nd TFW, 23rd TFS, SP tail code, standard camouflage scheme

Super Scale, Sheet Number 48-076

This sheet provides Phantom stenciling in white.

Super Scale, Sheet Number 48-108

The same three RF-4Cs as listed for sheet 72-320 above are on this sheet in 1/48th scale.

Super Scale, Sheet Number 48-110

This sheet has markings for three RF-4Cs as listed for sheet 72-324 above.

Super Scale, Sheet Number 48-143

Markings for three Air National Guard RF-4Cs are included on this sheet.

RF-4C, 64-1050, Nebraska ANG, wraparound camouflage scheme

RF-4C, 65-828, Nebraska ANG, standard camouflage scheme, as marked for PHOTO FINISH '81

RF-4C, 64-1061, Minnesota ANG, CO's aircraft, wraparound camouflage scheme

Super Scale, Sheet Number 48-144

Two RF-4Cs in the wraparound camouflage scheme are the subjects for this sheet.

RF-4C, 65-897, Nevada ANG, PHOTO FINISH '81

RF-4C, 64-1063, Kentucky ANG, BEST PHOTO '82

Super Scale, Sheet Number 48-147

This sheet has markings for one F-4E and one F-4C. The F-4C is 66-7678 from the 4th TFW. It is in the standard camouflage scheme and has an SA tail code. The aircraft was flown by COL Chuck Yeager.

Super Scale, Sheet Number 48-148

Markings for an F-4G and one F-4D are provided on this sheet. The F-4D is 65-731, and it is the commander's aircraft from the 31st TFW. It is in the standard camouflage scheme and has a ZF tail code.

Super Scale, Sheet Number 48-155

Two F-4Cs are included on this sheet.

F-4C, 64-829, 482nd TFW, AFRES, standard camouflage scheme

F-4C, 63-7647, Hawaii ANG, standard camouflage scheme

Super Scale, Sheet Number 48-156

This sheet has markings for F-4C, 64-766, from the

Oregon ANG in the standard camouflage scheme and the later ADC Gray scheme. The aircraft has three MiG kills.

Super Scale, Sheet Number 48-161

Markings for one F-4C and two F-4Es are provided on this sheet. The F-4C is 63-7589, and it is from the 36th TFS of the 3rd TFW. It is painted in the standard camouflage scheme and has a UK tail code. A single MiG kill marking is on the inlet ramp.

Super Scale, Sheet Number 48-162

This sheet provides markings for an F-4C and an F-4E. The F-4C is 63-7413 from the 559th TFS of the 12th TFW. It is painted in the standard camouflage scheme, has an XN tail code, and is named BLUE AVENGER.

Super Scale, Sheet Number 48-167

An F-4D and an F-4E are on this sheet. The F-4D is 66-7554 from the 555th TFS of the 432rd TRW. It is painted in the standard camouflage scheme, has an OY tail code, and is named Trapper. It has a painting of Snoopy on its left air inlet.

Super Scale, Sheet Number 48-189

Two Air National guard F-4Cs are represented on this sheet. They include:

F-4C, 64-937, North Dakota ANG, standard camouflage scheme

F-4C, 63-7618, Michigan ANG, ADC Gray scheme

Super Scale, Sheet Number 48-194

This sheet provides markings for an F-4C and an F-4E. The F-4C is 63-7522, and it is from the 556th TFS of the 12th TFW. It is painted in the standard camouflage scheme, has an XT tail code, and is named SAINTLY SINNER.

Super Scale, Sheet Number 48-196

Three different types of Phantoms are on this sheet to include an F-4E, an F-4C, and an RF-4C. The F-4C and RF-4C are painted in the standard camouflage scheme and are marked as follows:

F-4C, 64-665, 12th TFW, 557th TFS, XC tail code, named HELL'S ANGEL

RF-4C, 65-870, 432nd TRW, OO tail code, named Hillbilly Slick (misidentified on sheet as an F-4C)

Super Scale, Sheet Number 48-197

Two F-4Cs and one F-4D in the standard camouflage scheme are represented on this sheet.

F-4C, 63-7584, 58th TFTW, commander's aircraft with black and white high visibility stripes, LA tail code

F-4C, 64-829, 8th TFW, 555th TFS, FG tail code, two MiG kills, named SCAT XXVII, flown by COL Robin Olds

F-4D, 66-7463, 555th TFS, OY tail code, flown by Steve Ritchie for his first and fifth kills

Super Scale, Sheet Number 48-249

This sheet has markings for one F-4C and one F-4D.

F-4C, 64-841, Louisiana ANG, unique two tone gray camouflage scheme

F-4D, 66-7466, Minnesota ANG, ADC Gray scheme

Super Scale, Sheet Number 48-253

Three different Air National Guard markings are on this sheet which includes two F-4Cs and one F-4D.

F-4C, 63-7423, California ANG, wraparound scheme

F-4C, 63-7704, Louisiana ANG, special two tone gray scheme, one MiG kill on inlet ramp

F-4D, 66-7745, Alabama ANG, European 1 camouflage scheme with AL tail code

Super Scale, Sheet Number 48-272

Four F-4Cs and one F-4D are included on this sheet.

F-4C, 63-7583, Michigan ANG, ADC Gray scheme, named Garfield or Never Trust A Smiling Cat

F-4C, 63-7442, Michigan ANG, ADC Gray scheme, named Baby (misidentified as 63-7583 on instruction sheet which is for aircraft immediately above)

F-4C, 63-7626, Michigan ANG, ADC Gray scheme, named No More Mr. Nice Guy

F-4C, 63-7702, Texas ANG, ADC Gray scheme

F-4D, 66-7554, 906th TFG, AFRES, European 1 scheme, DO tail code, named City of Fairborn

Super Scale, Sheet Number 314

This sheet is the 1/48th scale equivalent to sheet 72-541 covered above. It also has the problem with the gray markings being too light, thus making the markings for F-4D, 66-7681, unusable.

Super Scale, Sheet Number 445

Markings for three RF-4Cs are provided on this sheet. They are the same as on sheet 72-659 covered above.

War Eagle, Sheet Number 1

This limited run sheet provides markings for F-4C, 63-7534. It was from the Michigan ANG, was painted in the ADC Gray scheme, and was named DEFIANCE II.

Xtradecal, Sheet Number X004 48

This sheet has markings for four U-2/TR-1 aircraft and one RF-4C. The RF-4C is 68-567, and it is from the 1st TRS of the 10th TRW. It has an AR tail code and is painted in the European 1 camouflage scheme.

1/32nd SCALE SHEETS

It should be noted that as of this writing, there are no kits of the F-4C or F-4D available in 1/32nd scale.

Aerodecal, Sheet Number 26B

This sheet has the same markings as Aerodecal sheet number 25A which is covered above.

Super Scale, Sheet 32-030

Markings for two F-4Es and one F-4C are included on this sheet. The F-4C is misidentified as an F-4D on the instructions. It is F-4C, 63-7470 from the 67th TFS of the 18th TFW. The standard camouflage scheme is used on the aircraft, along with a ZG tail code. The unusual but understandable name of this Phantom is Rub-A-Dub-Dub, two men in a tub. The instructions state that the modeler should add a sensor to the F-4J kit, but much more work would have to be done to convert an F-4J to an F-4C or F-4D.